The  MBA Blueprint for Success

How to maximise your career opportunities

G Harrison

The MBA Blueprint for Success

by

G Harrison

Published by BRY Publishing

Copyright © G Harrison, 2020

G Harrison asserts the moral right to be identified as the author of this work.

All rights reserved.

Without limiting the rights under copyright reserved above, no part of this publication may be reproduced, stored in or introduced into a retrieval system, or transmitted, in any form or by any means (electronic, mechanical, photocopying, recording or otherwise), without the prior written consent of both the copyright owner and the publisher of this book.

Thank you for respecting the hard work of this author.

ISBN: 978-1-913742-99-7

Why this book was written:

The MBA Blueprint for Success demystifies the Master of Business Administration degree, providing an honest and balanced guide to help you understand how you can make an MBA work for you. From unravelling the hype that goes along with MBAs to the hidden aspects that business schools and MBA graduates would never usually freely admit to, this book is an easy to follow, step-by-step guide on everything you need to consider for your journey.

Ten years before graduating from one of the world's leading business schools with an MBA with distinction, I set out on what looked to be an extremely ambitious journey at the time. Starting out in debt and with none of the prerequisites for an MBA programme, I methodically and consistently worked through what needed to be done to improve my own personal situation by securing an MBA. However, once I reached the prestigious goal, I noticed that many who considered a similar path were put off by their perceptions of MBAs, whether it would be too difficult, too expensive, or what they would actually get from having one. Having experienced these perspectives during my own journey, I began to ask my friends and colleagues about their own experiences. It quickly became apparent that there were a range of common misconceptions held by people who were considering pursuing an MBA. For some of these people, these misconceptions would completely deter them from pursuing an MBA as a way to improve their professional and personal situation. It was this awareness and desire to help those in similar circumstances that led me to pull together these insights, knowledge and first-hand experience from an extensive global network, including MBA alumni from a world-leading MBA course, as well as a range of university, recruitment and industry contacts.

This is why the MBA Blueprint for Success was written – to help anyone who is willing to commit and consistently work hard to improve their situation, and in doing so, maximise their personal and professional opportunities.

About the author:

This book is purposely written with a level of anonymity for myself, my MBA network and contacts in a wide range of university, recruitment and industry roles. The insights from this extensive global network are encapsulated and presented throughout the book as a single, coherent perspective. This anonymity is there to ensure I felt free enough to write about my experiences and could also provide this freedom of expression to those I spoke with, enabling honest and unbiased views on MBAs to be presented.

The MBA Blueprint for Success

Contents

Introduction

Getting the most out of this book

Chapter One: MBA Myths

1.1 You will become an expert in business
1.2 There are other ways of replicating the knowledge and experience
1.3 You will be learning from the best
1.4 Getting an MBA will automatically increase your leadership skills
1.5 Networking in your cohort should always be a top priority
1.6 Reputation of the university and business school doesn't matter
1.7 A more expensive MBA provides more value
1.8 You will achieve the advertised average post-graduation salary automatically
1.9 Summary

Chapter Two: The Application Process

2.1 What schools look for in applicants
2.2 Developing an application

2.3 Developing your CV/resume
2.4 Employer references
2.5 Bias in the process

Chapter Three: The MBA Demographic, Networking and Reputation

3.1 The MBA demographic
3.2 Networking internally versus externally
3.3 Internal versus external professional reputation

Chapter Four: Full-time, Part-time, Online?

4.1 Weighing it up – positives and negatives

Chapter Five: Prioritisation and Planning

5.1 Priorities
5.2 Time, family life and relationships
5.3 Opportunity cost and funding

Chapter Six: Content Overview from a World-Leading MBA

6.1 Content overview
6.2 Specialisms and your expectations

Chapter Seven: Increase Your Chances of Getting Good Marks

7.1 Criticality
7.2 Tutor bias
7.3 Collaboration
7.4 Methods of assessment
7.5 Effort versus goals

Chapter Eight: Maximising Your Opportunities Before, During and After Your MBA

8.1 Before your MBA
8.2 During your MBA
8.3 After your MBA

Chapter Nine: Pulling it All Together

9.1 Conclusion: How to make an MBA work for you

The MBA Blueprint for Success

Introduction

Wherever you are in your own journey, there is always something you can work on to improve your situation.

This ultimate belief led to the creation of this book, with MBAs often presenting a strong route to enabling improvement in your own situation. The applications of this can be broad and might apply whether your goal is to improve the type of work you do in itself, a way of pursuing higher pay, increased seniority or pursuing a different career altogether. This book will help you in this journey by delving into the pros and cons of getting an MBA and what the true journey of achieving one involves. After a ten year journey to achieving an MBA with distinction from one of the world's leading business schools, I call on both my first-hand experience and the experience of others in my network, sharing insights that business schools and MBA graduates would never usually freely admit to. These insights will help you to make the most informed decision you possibly can based on your situation and help you to maximise your career opportunities.

Many falsely believe that unless you go to an elite business school, an MBA is simply not worth it due to the assumption that employers value MBAs from less prestigious universities much less favourably. This is an unfortunate misconception because it often puts people off from even trying or completely cuts off an MBA as a possible route to furthering their success. There are so many alternative business schools out there that may not be the top of the global league tables but are still leaders in business education. These can provide great value for money and return on investment for many career paths. My network is full of success stories from individuals who attended business schools that aren't from the very top of global league tables and who studied through a range of modes of study (such as online, part-time or full-time). There are a few exceptions which we will come onto but generally, achieving your career aspirations is often down to having the right approach, commitment and hard work rather than whether your business school was ranked at the very top of league tables.

Although many potential MBA students will be pursuing an MBA to secure higher seniority and the increased pay that goes along with this, there are a whole host of other reasons students look to complete MBAs. These can range from wanting to improve specific aspects of society, through improvement where government interfaces with businesses, to enabling charities to have greater impact and success. Many students also seek the skills MBAs teach and the chance to network extensively as a way of gaining independence from conventional employment, by using their new insights and skills to support them in starting their own businesses in the best possible way. So although this book is mostly framed as helping you to maximise your career opportunities, this isn't necessarily always about making more money and instead can just as easily be translated into making more of a difference in the world than you might otherwise have had the opportunity to. Many of the people who I had the pleasure of sharing my MBA experience with were from non-governmental organisations, charities, local and central government and non-profit healthcare organisations. For these people, having a greater impact in their work and making the world a better place was their primary goal and the MBA helped them to achieve this through enhancing their skills and enabling them to drive improvement quickly and effectively.

One thing you might not have come to realise yet is that those seeking, working towards, completing and holding an MBA can often polarise other people in the workplace. They can stir up emotions in others on whether they've reached their own goals and fulfilled their potential or are getting the recognition they deserve for their work rather than credentials. Whilst the focus behind this attention may originate in the perceptions of others, pursuing an MBA will undoubtedly mean people will begin to notice you more in your workplace. Used positively, this attention can in turn allow you to begin to raise your profile and build your personal brand, through demonstrating your enhanced capabilities over time. As well as raising your profile more broadly, you may also find you are able to create much stronger professional links with others who have this qualification and others who may want to pursue it.

There are a whole host of reasons behind the positive and negative reactions you might initially receive when the topic of MBAs come up, most of which will be out of your control. Some of these reactions are likely to originate in the elite status which can come from having an MBA and the doors it can (fairly or unfairly) unlock for you to open. However, the key in all of this is perception – in many cases, MBAs aren't much more than a badge of competence, albeit a very expensive one.

Although their popularity can vary between people and companies, as well as changing over time, many job roles continue to keep them as desirable or essential requirements, resulting in them continuing to hold value for countless industries and positions. The value of holding an MBA is likely set to continue if you consider some of the cultural, technological, political, economic and environmental changes that we are seeing in the world. This is supported through data presented by the Our World in Data publication and summarised well by Calderon's work on the massification of higher education, both showing a general increasing trend for global degree-level education, beyond the pace of our global population growth[1,2,3]. Although the data shows there are differences between global regions in the level of growth, it does reflect the ability of MBAs to provide a further level of differentiation above those holding undergraduate degrees. Over time, this differentiation is likely to become increasingly more important, particularly for some industries and positions. This is because as more and more people possess advanced degrees such as MBAs, there is a good chance they will come to be increasingly expected over time in the industries that continue to hold them as requirements. Despite these increasing expectations, the ability you develop to differentiate yourself well will continue to allow you to reap the rewards MBAs can provide.

This book aims to help you by combing the experiences from my own specific journey as well as the shared insights from others who attended business school before, at the same time, and after my own MBA. This is compiled into one easy to read, step-by-step guide intended to give you a strong general understanding of the MBA landscape which can be applied to your specific situation. Although this is written as a single perspective, this is most certainly not one individual viewpoint. It is the collection of the thoughts and inputs from extensive discussions with tens of contributors, representing a huge

---

[1] https://ourworldindata.org/grapher/projection-of-world-population-ssp2-iiasa?time=2020..2100
[2] https://ourworldindata.org/future-population-growth#the-world-population-by-educational-structure
[3] https://www.researchgate.net/publication/331521091_Massification_of_higher_education_revisited

variety of academic and industry experience, as well as social and cultural backgrounds.

By the end of this book, you should have a better idea of whether an MBA is for you and if it is, how you can maximise your career opportunities.

Getting the most out of this book

Although the book is split into distinct sections, each detailing key aspects to consider and how to maximise the opportunities presented to you, many elements are interlinked. If you prioritise one aspect, it may impact another and so on. Depending on your own circumstances and priorities, some parts of the book may be more important to you but there will likely be many interrelationships at play in the decisions you need to make. Therefore, this book is most beneficial when read in its entirety as this will encourage you to take a holistic view, based on the variety of considerations we will explore.

If you're looking to get the holistic view of the book condensed as much as possible, at the end of the book in Chapter Eight, there is a helpful summary which pulls everything together on how to maximise your opportunities at each stage of the journey: before, during and after your MBA. This details what to think about and how you might want to prioritise your approach in targeting business schools and modes of study based on your priorities, if you come to the conclusion that pursuing an MBA might help you improve your situation. The main body of the book will give you more detail on how to make the most of the opportunity with summaries at the end of each part.

Chapter One

MBA Myths

Chapter One covers some of the common myths and misconceptions around MBAs, from the realisations of both myself and others as to what an MBA truly means in real terms to the benefit having one will actually bring you.

1.1 You will become an expert in business

You're more than likely already aware that MBAs are a master's degree level qualification. They can be difficult to achieve, requiring sustained academic rigour and demonstrable soft skills. However, most courses cover so many topics in such a short space of time that you simply don't have time to become an expert in any aspect of the course. What MBAs are good at is giving you an overview of business at a high level - think generalist rather than specialist.

There are definite advantages to MBAs being a generalist degree, as to become an effective business leader, you will need a good understanding of a wide range of business aspects. The aim is to appreciate a wide range of business concepts without necessarily needing to know them in great detail. Your understanding needs to just be enough to appreciate what subject matter experts may engage with you on in order to be able to make more informed decisions in interconnected and complex broad business areas.

This general business acumen is what MBA courses are designed to help you develop and by learning about business aspects you may not have previously come into much contact with, it can open up your curiosity to new areas you may enjoy or find a new direction in. This is also why MBAs can be used to begin a change in career direction. However, the flip side to this is that due to their generalist nature, demonstrating true experience in the new direction can be difficult without relevant pre-MBA experience or MBAs offering an internship in the areas you're looking to transition into. Even with internships in specific areas, you will very likely still not be considered anything close to an expert in anything specific by the end of the course. This is why although MBAs can be used to begin a change in career direction, the beginning of this change post-graduation is likely to be a lot lower down in seniority than you may hope.

Although course content varies by business school, it will usually follow roughly the same general core subjects. Depending on the individual university, these may be labelled slightly differently or combined into groups, but in essence will cover the same fundamental topics:

- Leadership
- Management
- Human Resource Management
- Finance and Accounting
- Economics
- Strategy
- Marketing
- Operations Management
- Technology

Some universities will have optional modules which can be more easily changed to fit demand, available specialist lecturers and any emerging concepts. These may go into more skill-based areas such as Project Management or Change Management. Alternatively, they might include modules like Entrepreneurship, Innovation or Data, although the emphasis of these often vary by university and may depend on the interests and specialisms of professors at the business schools. You may find that these optional modules explore specific areas within a broad subject, such as solely focusing on start-up creation within Entrepreneurship. Although this presents an opportunity to go more in-depth, it also comes with risk as it will likely be based on the specialisms and potential biases of a single professor. If it's done well and is what you're interested in, it could be great and if not, it could end up being a wasted choice of a module.

Irrespective of whether you pursue a generalist or a more specialist MBA, the skills you will develop will still be universally applicable and allow you to develop your own capabilities at an accelerated rate. Much of the emphasis of MBAs is placed on developing softer skills, including communication and leadership, through team working, discussion and networking. As a result, the course content and experience of those attending relies heavily on the capabilities and input of the cohort. This is part of the reason behind the entry criteria requiring specific experience and prior education: everyone needs to bring their prior experiences to the table and everyone must have something to offer.

Many of those attending my own business school had the misplaced expectation they would be learning ground-breaking new business theories but were surprised and disappointed to find out we were learning about theories from decades ago. However, by being disheartened at this realisation they sometimes missed the point, as much of the benefit and true learning came through discussion in applying those theories to modern situations. Similarly, many concepts can be packaged as new but are often just slightly redesigned approaches of the past. One of many examples of this included the application of glocalisation within business environments (for example a globally distributed product which is tailored to local consumer markets, such as HSBC's local advertisement focus within its branding as the world's local bank). This concept has been around since the early 1990's and on the face of it might be old news to some. However, this practice continues to be adopted by businesses with great success and is as relevant today as it was when it began to be adopted. The evolution of this practice in an ever-increasing globalised world is just one example of where the next challenges might arise for businesses, in attempting to make products as desirable as possible across increasingly well-connected global mass markets.

During an MBA, most of your own understanding of current emerging themes and technological capabilities will come from the real-world and live experience of the cohort rather than academics who might not have worked outside of academia for five or ten years. This diversity of experience within the cohort is a large part of the real benefit of an MBA, whether you're looking at how best to embed a new product in a complex market landscape or overcoming difficult leadership challenges, everyone has a different view based on their experience. This leads the discussion into some interesting concepts and potential solutions about how to address complex business issues; it is the ability to approach and overcome complex issues in a holistic and balanced way that can be such a sought after skill for MBA graduates. Many professors and business schools generally will be open and honest about this skill being primarily developed through the cohort discussion and interaction rather than their course content, but this openness does vary. Understanding that you won't become an expert in business but instead understanding what you will gain and how you will gain it will help you to sell your experience both internally and externally within your professional environment. This leads us into the next related myth.

1.2 There are other ways of replicating the knowledge and experience

Now you might begin to wonder if I've swallowed the marketing blurb of business schools and their hype but hear me out. Business schools continue to exist in part because they offer a unique experience. No self-taught course, fast-track short course, or company training is going to be able to properly replicate the experience gained through an MBA. At best, these will be able to replicate a very small part or element of a typical course. This largely comes back to the soft skill development within such a diverse environment as a result of the diversity of the cohort, but also due to the way you develop skills whilst working through the sustained and in-depth experience as a whole.

Many of these skills need time and consistency to properly form. For example, this might come through prioritisation skills developed through working under continued pressure. Similarly, your exposure to, and demonstration of, consistent higher and critical levels of thinking over a sustained period of time are also required to get the most out of the MBA experience. Everyone learns differently but almost everyone benefits greatly from the engagement and interaction provided by each individual in the cohort, ultimately helping everyone to consider and apply solutions to complex problems in dynamic environments. Due to this style of consistent collaboration with others and level of sustained personal development over time, it is extremely difficult to replicate this in other settings which often follow a less rigorous approach.

Many MBA students come out of the MBA experience with a newfound sense of capability as a result of how intense the courses have been and how much they achieved in a short space of time, which isn't something that is easily replicated outside of the traditional setting. An element of this personal confidence may be down to the hype which is instilled in students on leaving business school on the value of the MBA they have received. However, even if we assume there is an element of false confidence at work, there is something to be said for this confidence boost, artificially inflated or not. What this confidence boost is worth and whether you personally might be able to replicate this specific aspect through other means, if it's an important part of your development needs, is another question.

In terms of replicating the knowledge gained on MBA courses, much of the content is readily available online if you're willing to do the searching and put in the time to reading and absorbing it. However, the interaction element is what embeds this knowledge in business school. Over the course of a module, there are a huge range of literature and concepts covered and sometimes there will be too much for even the most dedicated student to absorb. The priority and purpose of the MBA is developing your ability to quickly and effectively compare and contrast these and engage with the cohort and lecturers in the context of real-world problems. This way of intensively acquiring real-world business knowledge and understanding is difficult to replicate outside of a business school setting, as it would usually otherwise occur at a much slower pace. The vast amount of information and perspectives covered can be overwhelming. However, MBA courses are highly effective at structuring this learning process in such a way that makes the journey and learning experience as smooth and consistent as possible.

What the overall business school and MBA experience is worth in terms of value to you personally will vary depending on your circumstances and aspirations and we'll go into more depth on this in the following chapters. We'll also explore the different range of experiences available when undertaking an MBA (full-time, part-time and online), each of which holds its own unique pros and cons.

1.3 You will be learning from the best

This will depend on the business school, and will undoubtedly vary and could be subjective, but it is likely you will often have tutors who are very academically experienced but may have very limited relevant or recent real-world business experience. This can lead to some interesting disagreements between MBA students and professors and sometimes general dissatisfaction in the course content or teaching from the cohort.

In the experience of my cohort and business school, most professors recognised the experience of the cohort and leveraged this to use those experiences to build on teaching material, but taking the experiences of others in other business schools, unfortunately this is not always the case. As an example from my own experience, on one occasion, the cohort experience was so diverse and added so much value to the base content of the module that the tutor sacrificed teaching the last part of the base content in detail to spend more time in discussion. This was right for that specific situation but goes to show that there is a strong relationship and co-dependency between course content and cohort input.

In fact, much of the benefit of MBA courses comes from discussion-based learning within modules and good universities recognise and facilitate this. Some of the worst experiences and less-productive sessions within our business school came from when professors relied too heavily on their own limited to no industry experience and held strong views, which often contrasted with some of the views of students. It was a difference in understanding of the rationale behind their positions which led to the disagreements, with neither student nor professor being willing to spend more time understanding this difference in more depth. Being open to understanding new perspectives is a fundamental requirement to successfully achieving an MBA and making the most of the experience. Although the close-mindedness of others will hopefully be the exception for you, it does occur both in business schools and the general workplace and you should clearly be wary of this and look to overcome it where you find it.

1.4 Getting an MBA will automatically increase your leadership skills

MBAs will not automatically turn you into a leader or increase your leadership skills without your continual focus both during and after the course. Being open to learning and growing is a key part of this continuous journey. I saw many examples of those in our business school who came in with fixed mindsets and left with exactly the same attitude and beliefs and, I would argue, no greater leadership than when they arrived. If the confidence that often goes along with holding an MBA turns to arrogance, they may even be less of a leader than when they started and it is these people who often give MBA graduates a bad reputation in the workplace.

MBA courses will generally show you different perspectives and case studies on leadership, allowing you to analyse and make your own mind up, demonstrating critical thought on the actions of others in challenging situations. However, due to the reputation aspect of MBAs, there will be others that assume the course content and experience is heavy on leadership development and depending on your aspirations and circumstances, you might be able to use this perception to your advantage. This could be your employer, a potential employer or those in your extended external network outside of the MBA. As leadership can also be somewhat subjective in some ways, this reputational belief of those holding MBAs being more capable leaders may also allow you to assume this notion until you begin being recognised as a leader.

After all, everyone can be a leader through their actions no matter what title or position in life they hold.

1.5 Networking in your cohort should always be a top priority

As with all social situations in life, you will naturally get on with some people more than others and the same is true within in an MBA cohort. It's vital to remember that it isn't just your direct cohort that contributes to your network: all alumni, current colleagues and connections you've made socially and professionally are also valuable relationships.

Although you will graduate with an automatic network of sorts, as with all networking, you will need to nurture and grow these meaningful and mutually beneficial relationships in order for you to utilise their full potential. As so many people are conditioned to believe in how important this networking aspect of MBAs is, the environment can feel forced during the course, adding pressure to an already high-workload and sometimes stressful experience. This can include specific networking events ran by the university such as lunches and social events, with guest speakers or skill development activities. During these demanding times, where these networking events coincide with deadlines, it can be worthwhile taking a step back to evaluate your priorities. There are times when you may find it more beneficial to use the time that could be spent networking to work on other aspects of the course.

The importance of networking shouldn't be ignored, particularly for some roles and industries, but the value of networking within the cohort is likely to be dependent on your reasons for pursuing the MBA in the first place. Bearing this in mind when you're networking with others in the cohort is important. You may encounter some students who may not be overly interested in this aspect if it doesn't fit with their individual nature, personal priorities, or reasons behind doing an MBA. This is one of the reasons why it's a good idea to find out what others' motivations were for pursuing an MBA within your own business school. There is a balance here, with some people understanding a need for this balance and others less so, as those within this latter group can often place a comparatively higher priority on networking within the cohort. This is completely fine but worth considering when your own time is under pressure and you need to make the balance between building effective working relationships and meeting your deadlines with work of a good standard.

1.6 Reputation of the university and business school doesn't matter

The importance of institutional reputation will heavily depend on your individual circumstances and will be a factor in the cost benefit analysis you will need to do when considering your available options in pursuing an MBA. If you want an MBA purely to have a tick in the box for job applications, then the reputation of the specific business school may matter less than if you want to use a business school with a more prestigious reputation to give you an enhanced competitive edge. Similarly, the importance of the reputation will vary depending on the types of industry and role you're pursuing.

Generally, the more prominent the university and course status, the harder it will be to get accepted onto an MBA course as the university will want to maintain and grow their standing. For every applicant, they will need to assess the likelihood that you'll be able to continue to build that reputation on graduating, supporting the positive feedback cycle that forms the basis of the MBA Blueprint for Success. Universities benefit because they continue to build their position against competing universities, attract better professors, take on more students or students of a higher calibre and charge higher fees. You benefit because you have access to a better network and command higher salaries and better jobs as a result of their reputation and the experience you've gained.

If you're early on in your career and looking to progress, having a university with a better, more prestigious status on your CV can rightly or wrongly put you ahead of other applicants. This will depend on industry, role and the hiring manager but may help in making your first impressions with potential employers or with hiring managers in your own company. This is described by MBA career coaches as building a halo effect around you: the better each aspect of your employment history, education and experience, the more effective your halo is at providing a better, higher impact first impression. If you're self-employed and pursuing an MBA to build more holistic business knowledge to help you improve your company, you will likely be interested in looking at business schools that have a track record of high-quality teaching and as a result, reputation will still likely matter.

Generally, whatever your reasons are for pursuing an MBA, a better reputation will put you in a better position so my advice would be to assess low cost, less prestigious universities out there objectively against your goals and whether these match. Make sure you do as much research as you can into alumni and their journeys in your chosen field or field you want to progress into and don't just rely on the alumni stories posted by the universities - these are likely to be people with close ties to the business school and will more than likely be more biased than your average student. Alumni in your chosen field are a good place to start in verifying if reputation matters for your chosen career path.

1.7 A more expensive MBA provides more value

This is a tricky one, for a few reasons. A business school offering a more expensive MBA may be able to brand itself as offering a superior product, which may attract a more well-off student who is able to afford the extortionate fees. In turn, this can have a positive feedback on the university's student outcomes post-graduation. This can be due to the fact that if the cohort is made up of a mix of these more well-off students in the first place, they're likely to be well connected outside of the university network and naturally more likely to end up in high paying, high profile jobs. Similar to the situation with those attending Oxford and Cambridge universities in the UK, for some students, part of the appeal of attending such an institution is attending alongside future prime ministers and high powered executives and by proxy, expanding your network to include those people.

However, value for money is subjective and dependent on your goals. There are clear ranges in terms of price for MBA courses. The choice of university is going to depend on your own desired outcomes and may be location or industry dependent. Very roughly, at the time of writing, some of the less prestigious universities in the UK are offering MBAs for less than around £15,000. For ease of comparison, at the time of writing, this approximately equates to $20,000. Most of the more respected UK universities range from around £25,000 to £60,000 (equating to approximately $33,000 to $80,000), with some universities charging even more than this upper range. Outside of the UK, these numbers can be much greater, with MBAs from prestigious universities in the US costing well in excess of $150,000, whilst Europe's prestigious universities generally fall into the $50,000 to $100,000 range.

As we covered in the previous myth, despite their high cost, MBAs are often seen as a badge and their value thrives off reputation. This value is often clearly demonstrated in financial terms through return on investment. The average salary increase seen by students from prior to starting their MBA to three years following graduation was recorded as a 114% increase by the Financial Times in 2020[4]. This particular data pulls information from across the top 100 global MBAs and represents a wide range of MBA course costs and modes of study (full-time, part-time, online). A more respected university, higher in league tables or respected in industry, is more likely to present you with greater opportunities for larger salary increases than a less respected one. This is supported by the same data from the Financial Times, which shows the top 50 global MBAs to have had an average salary increase of 127% and the bottom 50 global MBAs to have had an average salary increase of 101%.

Despite this difference between more and less prestigious universities, the increase remains remarkable if we assume this increase is largely attributable to the MBA. It's worth appreciating that these figures are likely to be heavily influenced by more prestigious schools being more selective of their candidates in the first place as well as there being a wide range of variables at play, including the predominant industries and geographies represented

---

[4] http://rankings.ft.com/businessschoolrankings/global-mba-ranking-2020

and targeted by the cohort. Universities often release this information on both pre- and post-MBA average salaries for their courses, which may provide more of a detailed guide to the potential financial benefits you could see when graduating from specific institutions. However, as we have mentioned, these need to be closely considered in tandem with the characteristics of the cohort, individuals and your own characteristics, to fully understand if this insight might be influenced by any key variables and are realistic to apply in your own situation.

You might think a more prestigious university providing better value is obvious after reading the above. However, there are a range of cheaper alternatives available to getting MBAs in less respected (and still very effective) universities which may actually present better value for money for your career aspirations and personal situation. These alternative better value courses may suit your goals or needs better, or you may have restrictions on funding to consider – not everyone can or might want to afford $100,000 or more to go to a prestigious business school. Similarly, it may be worth paying more if you're not willing or unable to compromise on certain elements of courses offered in other institutions you're considering. This decision is a personal one and needs to be made depending on what value you think you would get from having that specific business school on your CV in the future against a whole host of other considerations, covered in much more detail through the rest of this book.

As well as the average salary increase information available, you may also be able to access pre-defined value for money scores in league tables. However, it's worth bearing in mind that any value for money scores you find will be generic and won't consider your own priorities and situation. In determining the value for money in your specific circumstances, if you can, it's worth speaking to those who have already completed the MBA at that institution and not necessarily just those who are designated alumni ambassadors or speakers for the university. It's worth also considering the roles you want to pursue, the companies and industry you want to work in as well as any locational factors. The more information you can gather to make your decision, the better. This is a complex decision and this book is going to dive into these often interlinked factors to help you consider aspects which you might not have considered.

1.8 You will achieve the advertised average post-graduation salary automatically

Another myth which I'm sure won't surprise you is that the average post-graduation salary advertised by the business school won't materialise without hard work outside of the MBA from you. This probably sounds like a really obvious statement but several of those within my cohort joked about the fact that after graduating, they still weren't anywhere near the average post-graduation salary, which had been quite heavily advertised in the marketing material. They saw the advertised figures as a bit of a pipe dream or somehow unrealistic, but in reality, they were doing little to affect a change in their career position and were unwilling to compromise on aspects of their lifestyle or employment.

The advertised average post-graduation salary and average percentage increases will vary from business school to business school and of course, year to year. Generally, they range from just below 50% and can claim as much as over 200%, with the time period being taken from the point you apply to three years after graduation. The trouble with these advertised figures is they're averages and are often provided with limited context of the cohort or how they were calculated. Both also need to be viewed in tandem, as a percentage increase on an already large number may be smaller but may show you what salary level you're starting from in comparison to the rest of the cohort. It goes without saying that the lower your starting salary, the higher potential you will have to increase that number by a large percentage.

Your opportunities to increase your salary will heavily depend on your own unique employment situation and as a result, if advancing your income is your primary goal, this may require you to leave your current company or move locations in some circumstances. Either way, progress will require you to maximise the potential from your MBA experience. Many universities offer free career coaching to support you in this, both during and after the course, and can connect you with alumni who may be able to help support through providing advice or opportunities. In addition to alumni, you will also have your network from within your own cohort and the external connections you may have made through your MBA journey. It is this network and support that can be so valuable as part of doing an MBA.

1.9 Summary

Although some of these myths and misconceptions may appear negative, there are a lot of positives to be gained from doing an MBA. It might be one of the most expensive purchases and biggest commitments in your life, but this is often worthwhile and can open up opportunities that wouldn't have been possible otherwise. In fact, I would go as far to say that if it fits with your career and personal development plan, you're ambitious and you are willing to accept you may need to change to get to where you want to be, it can be transformative and even life-changing. As part of this, you will need to push yourself and continually move out of your comfort zone but if you do, you're almost certain to grow in ways you likely won't even have foreseen.

Now I realise that the MBA experiences of myself and my network compiled to create this book may present some bias, but the following sections were created to purposefully explore both the positives and negatives, including how to make the best of situations where negatives may be presented. Both myself and many of those in my network are under no illusion - there are many potential challenges and negative aspects to consider when pursuing and undertaking an MBA.

This book is here to help you think about whether it will realistically fit your life and your goals and if it does, there are definite steps you can take to maximise the potential you have to further your career and make the MBA Blueprint for Success work for you. This is a win-win scenario: the more money students make post-graduation and the more impact they have in the world, the more money the business schools make and round the cycle goes. This situation makes for a great opportunity for those who want to take it as far as they can, if making money, being successful and having an impact on your life and the world is your ambition.

I also realise that not everyone's ambition is to make as much money as possible and this is perfectly fine. There were plenty of people in my business school from charities, non-governmental organisations, family businesses, non-profit healthcare organisations and local and central governments. For some of these people, having an impact on the world was their primary goal and this is just as important, if not more so, in a world with ever-growing disparities between the rich and the poor.

Following bad press in the past, particularly around the time of the financial crisis, some business schools have tried to shake images of their cohorts feeding corporate capitalist companies with graduates who have questionable morals and money-grabbing tendencies, with schools increasingly including ethics as part of many modules. You'll be able to quite easily work out and decide for yourself if the business schools you're looking at are doing this to pay lip service to the idea or are genuinely invested in it. But overall, if students go on to have a positive impact in the world which isn't financially driven, this is just as well received (if not more so in some cases) and so continues the win-win scenario for students and the university.

Chapter Two

The Application Process

2.1 What schools look for in applicants

As covered in some of our common myths and misconceptions, by setting the bar high, business schools use positive bias to their advantage. There are a range of attributes and existing skills and capabilities business schools look for when selecting candidates. These include a compelling reason behind you pursuing the MBA (demonstrating passion and commitment), strong management and leadership experience, academic and professional achievement (including career trajectory and progression), personal integrity, energy and a willingness to learn. The extent to which these are weighted in the assessment for you as an individual will highly depend on your personal circumstances, the school itself and your ability to influence those assessing you as a potential candidate. This is certainly not a time to be modest or sell yourself short!

Before we get into how you can demonstrate some of these required attributes, skills and capabilities to help you meet the criteria, there is one aspect which often has a high degree of influence on the success of your application: your reason for pursuing the MBA. Competition for MBA places can be really high and it is your motivation for your application and your story behind this that can often make you stand out. Through this, you can provide a compelling narrative to show you are exactly the type of student the university is looking for. For the best chances of success, this needs to align to the values of the business school, your own values and demonstrate how you having an MBA from that specific business school will help both your career and the school. This is no small order but if done right, will give the university no reason not to accept you and every reason to welcome you as a student. This might sound strange as a concept, but by minimising any potential negative aspects of your application and enhancing the positive aspects as much as possible, you present yourself as a balanced and highly favourable potential candidate for the business school.

Business schools will be looking for a mixture of prior experience and capability as well as a passion to learn more about business. This could either be learning in greater depth and/or potentially new areas not yet explored, but which you might have an interest in. There is nothing wrong with seeking a more holistic business understanding if you have specialist work experience through a specific industry or role. Having a balance of being able to add value to the MBA cohort through existing knowledge and experience, whilst also having the potential to gain from the experience and progress further following the course, is what characterises most MBA students. However, you should be able to clearly state whatever it is you want from the course, what you want to gain from the whole experience and how you see it fitting within your future goals and helping you to achieve these, however ambitious they may be.

Once you have a good idea of how an MBA might professionally benefit you, by working in a personal element to your rationale, you can begin to make your application stand out from the crowd. Business schools receive hundreds of applications from candidates who will likely all meet the criteria to varying extents, but what makes you stand out as a person? What is it that you can offer from a personal perspective? What is unique about your individual story and motivation? Try to spend some time reflecting on this to find something you believe will both work as part of your story and also be something the business school you're targeting is looking for. It may even be worth asking a couple of trusted family, friends or colleagues who are close to you for their reflections. To try and help you think this through, some unique aspects might be related to the following examples:

- Your ability to engage with others.
- Your ability to overcome personal or professional obstacles and serious setbacks and failure.
- Your achievements beyond what was expected of you at the time.
- Your extra-curricular abilities that translate to the business world.

- A unique perspective you have as a result of your past experience.

These are just some of many possible examples. Once you have found something you think encapsulates you as a person, as well as also being something the business school would value, think more around how you can create a compelling story of how your strengths have provided advantage to you and others. In particular, think about the following points:

- Examples of when your abilities have resulted in high-impact results for you and/or others. What did this help you to learn about your abilities and how will this help the business school and you during your MBA?
- Examples of how you overcame specific personal or professional setbacks and learned from these to improve yourself and others further. How will your experience of these in the past help you and the business school as an MBA candidate?
- Examples of how your abilities may have differed to others and why this makes you particularly suited to being an MBA candidate at that specific business school. Can you generally see opportunities where others haven't? Have you been able to overcome issues that others have struggled with? If so, how did you effectively manage this to create value, deliver with impact and influence others? With an MBA, how might you be able to take this capability one step further and achieve greater things?

- How do your examples demonstrate your ambition and determination to succeed?

In thinking these examples and your story through, by relating them to that specific business school or MBA course, you can add a personalised element to your application and help add to your justification for applying. For example, does the university have strong links with an industry that aligns well with your capabilities? Does the business school or the research conducted by specific lecturers align with your values? Whatever the unique selling point of the business school or the lecturers, think about how you may be able to incorporate this into your story and rationale.

Moving on from your reason for applying to the specific MBA, now we'll take a look at some of the prerequisites you're likely to encounter and how you can demonstrate these even if you might initially think you don't meet the requirements.

Management and leadership experience

Many business schools require a certain number of years' experience at a managerial level. However, this can take a few forms, can be a little open to interpretation and might be somewhat flexible if you are willing to position your skills in a slightly creative way. We're not talking about lying or even exaggerating here but as an example, it might not mean needing direct line management experience if you can demonstrate you're working in a matrix structure and practising leadership and/or management through other means. This might be influencing the development of strategies, helping develop a culture of learning and innovation or doing the right thing in challenging situations.

Similarly, if you can demonstrate coaching or mentoring experience, with someone on your extended team or in your wider network, the school might interpret this as demonstrating management calibre competencies. This experience doesn't have to be official for you to be able to use it as an example. For example, you may have helped a friend or colleague with specific training or more generally with their career, by helping them see different perspectives or guiding them through a difficult situation. Depending on the situations you choose, you may be able to demonstrate leadership and can position these examples as such across the different areas of your application, covering letter and CV.

Although higher impact examples are preferable, taking an approach of sharing several smaller situations and the benefit you delivered through these may show your consistency in demonstrating this behaviour and can be used to highlight your potential as a candidate in this area. To try and demonstrate the management and leadership impact you've had, consider how your approaches affected others, how you have influenced and negotiated with others and through your actions, positively changed outcomes. All of these traits demonstrate your social skills, self-awareness and emotional intelligence. Try to make any connection between your actions and the result clear and leave no doubt that it was your involvement that influenced the outcome. This is a time for you to shine in your examples and although a team effort is great, your examples should specifically say how you as an individual improved a challenging situation. Remember: don't be modest!

Entrepreneurial spirit

Many business schools value entrepreneurial spirit. Several students in my cohort had this as some sort of experience they readily sold as part of their background. These included setting up their own businesses, pursuing consultancy work as a side job as well as investing in stocks and property to let. If you can include any experiences such as this with your application, it can be used to demonstrate courage, willingness to learn and your ability to challenge the norm. These are all useful traits for the university to gauge your potential future success once you've completed the course with your newfound skills and network. This is a skill you can both weave into your examples and also specifically detail as examples in their own right, encapsulating a range of sought-after traits in the process. Although many students in my own cohort had this experience, many also didn't, and it didn't hold them back. So, although it can be a useful aspect to add to an application, it is by no means an essential one.

Academic and professional achievement

Almost all business schools have a prerequisite around some form of academic achievement, whether it's an undergraduate degree at a certain level and / or GMAT (Graduate Management Admission Test) score. Many universities will also want some evidence of proficiency in English if this isn't your native language and is the language the MBA will be taught in. This is usually assessed through tests, such as the IELTS (International English Language Testing System). However, it may be enough to provide evidence that you're working in English-speaking business roles or hold some other English-speaking qualification. Similarly, academic prerequisites can sometimes be replaced by portfolios of professional work. As MBAs are a professionally orientated degree, enough management experience may provide a route onto the course, replacing the requirement for an undergraduate degree.

Each application will undoubtedly be judged on its own merits, with career trajectory being another key aspect business schools are likely to seek evidence of. Some schools might ask for a CV as part of your application including salary details for each of your prior roles to judge increasing experience and responsibility over time. Through this, they will be looking to see if this is likely to continue and if you're accepted onto the course, whether you'll be likely to show further salary progression and achieve a high potential post-graduation salary - many business schools use this as a key measure of success. They will be looking at this trajectory not just in monetary terms but also in terms of increasing responsibility over time, so it may help to try and write your application in this way, linking it into what value the MBA would provide for you and what value you can bring as an applicant to the MBA cohort. It may be worth considering if it would benefit you to declare any additional perks you had in previous roles as part of declaring salary if this is required, as declaring or not declaring these may help support the progression story you are trying to tell.

Business schools seeking candidates with prior experience doesn't just help in their post-graduate outcomes, it also supports the MBA experience for the rest of those in the cohort. It would be a bit of a false real-world learning environment if everyone on an MBA course came straight from their undergraduate degree courses. The real-world experience of the cohort is a key contributing factor to the learning and networking experience and so as part of your application you will need to specifically mention what is unique about you and your experience and what you would bring to the cohort.

The more professional experience you have, the better, as you'll be able to demonstrate that you have the range of experiences that would allow you to add value through sharing insights and examples. As well as quantity, the quality and variety of this experience is key. The more you're able to demonstrate any unique insights, the more favourably you will likely be received as a potential applicant. The next section on developing an application will go into more depth on how to do this.

However, if you find yourself in the favourable position of having plenty of management experience to call on, you also need to make sure that you can still demonstrate how the course would add value to you and your development. Most reputable universities still want to see this, despite the fact you will likely be a low risk, high potential benefit candidate for them. Aside from post-graduation salary, another key measure universities apply to themselves is drop-out rates and they will want to try and ensure those attending do complete the course as this is another good selling point for potential students.

Values

As business schools have developed their thinking around ethics and social values, your ability to demonstrate your own conscious efforts to make the world a better place will be received favourably. This could be demonstrated through volunteering, giving something back through mentoring or coaching or demonstrating positive personal values through going above and beyond to make a difference from a social perspective. Demonstrating integrity through doing the right thing is often a key attribute favoured by businesses and any examples where you may have done this or held others accountable for doing the right thing may help demonstrate both your own moral values as well as your leadership.

Passion, energy and a willingness to learn

In telling your story of what you have to offer and what you stand to gain through attending the specific business school in question, don't forget to try and convey a passion for the university and your desire for achieving an MBA with them. Universities receive countless applications – you need to try and make yours stand out. What makes you different? In conveying this, make sure you use your writing and, if you are invited to any sort of interview, your communication to portray your enthusiasm. High-energy candidates make for engaging and engaged members of the cohort, which is something the university will value.

*

Although the above represent the main traits observed by business schools, this list isn't exhaustive and each characteristic can be weighted differently depending on its desirability for the specific school. As a result, it can be very worthwhile speaking to someone in the admissions department at the business schools you're looking to apply for to find more out about what they're specifically looking for in candidates.

You can use this intelligence to position your application after gauging how important each of their criteria is for the school. For example, they may consider less than the stated academic requirements if you have held management positions in a few companies or for a long time. Alternatively, they may consider slightly less than the stated management experience if you can demonstrate leadership in positions you hold through activities you do in your spare time. You likely won't be able to establish the priority for each and every requirement but may be able to ask specific questions on aspects you're concerned about by framing it as you seeking advice.

Depending on the business school, the admissions department will often be willing to look at your CV before you begin your application and provide recommendation on your chance of success, which cohort you may be best suited to, or whether they may be looking for more experience in specific areas before you apply. You can then use this to both focus on any weaknesses in your current experience and tailor your future application to address any concerns there may have potentially been. This may not be a service the university offers as standard to potential applicants, so positioning it as a request for advice, whilst reiterating your enthusiasm for the course, may be your best approach in trying to gauge this.

Universities will have a general admissions email address and many business schools also provide contact details online for their individual members of staff, including those working in the admissions department. Both the general admissions email and individual contacts can be perfectly viable routes in seeking advice for your application. The more elite the business school and more competitive it is for a place, the less likely the school admissions staff may be to offer bespoke advice due to the wide range of highly qualified potential candidates applying in each intake. Despite this, it is still worth a try if you are looking for an overview or specific advice.

It should be noted that by asking for advice on your suitability, you may forego your option to apply immediately following any negative feedback. Although this wouldn't be official, it may reflect badly if you have asked for advice, only to then go against it when it wasn't the answer you were hoping for. Another option you can explore to understand your suitability compared to the requirements is through looking alumni up on LinkedIn to gauge the range of prior education, experience and types of roles people would have held at the time they were accepted onto the course. Similarly, some alumni may be willing to share advice on the admissions process for your target universities so it might be worth reaching out and expanding your network in this way. This can be a really useful way to gauge how much of a gap there may be between your current experience and the experience that may be expected as a minimum for applications.

However, in looking at the previous experience of alumni on LinkedIn, I would advise using caution and not necessarily taking all at face value. This should only be used as a rough gauge as experience may have had quite a lot of spin and exaggeration added, particularly in cases where there has been some time since they held the position. Not everyone does this, and it can rightly catch people out down the line. You'll be able to spot some of these quite easily (some can verge on the ridiculous - when you see these you will know), but in doing this background research, don't let anyone else's experience or credentials put you off – each application is individual.

As a final point, it's worth considering from a distance, what does your application say to you? What are your obvious strengths, weaknesses and opportunities? Is your application consistent in its message on what you bring as an individual, what you stand to gain and what you can bring to the business school during and following your studies? From an overall perspective, you're looking to demonstrate you have technical competence through hard skills, whether that's through your role or through existing academic qualifications. In addition to this, you're also looking to demonstrate your soft skills through your experience and examples of how you've worked with or led others to overcome obstacles and achieve goals. In the next section on developing an application, we'll further explore how you can present these qualities in a high-impact way throughout your application.

Key takeaway points – what schools look for in applicants:
- A compelling reason to undertake an MBA.
    - What you will gain based on your own personalised compelling story.
    - What you will bring to the cohort and university.
- Management and leadership experience.
- Entrepreneurial spirit.
- Academic and professional achievement, including career trajectory and progression.

- Values (ethics and social values).
- Passion, energy and willingness to learn.
- A good all-round application, demonstrating soft and hard skills.

2.2 Developing an application

Your application will usually need to include a cover letter and a CV, but there can be other elements required depending on your experience, which might include a portfolio of professional work. There may also be a general application form to pull out key elements from your CV and job history in a standard format. Whatever the specific requirements, these elements need to link together and have a cohesive flow, with the cover letter further explaining and highlighting key points from your CV and/or portfolio and why these make you an ideal candidate. If you need to include a portfolio of work, this should also be focused and spell out why the experience specifically supports your application.

Basically, you should be giving the university every reason to welcome you and no reasons not to accept you onto the course and it should be easy for them to see your value as a prospective student. As we mentioned in the last section, by giving the university no reason not to accept you, you focus on your weaknesses as well as your strengths – you're only as strong as your weakest link!

The initial selection will likely be a key criterion check against what the university specifies so if you don't meet the initial checks, you might not get much further. However, how strict this is will depend on university, how many applicants there are for the year you're applying, their capacity and their targets. Make sure you read the application information carefully and cover every requirement as much as you can.

Another aspect you may want to consider is that the method of study (full-time, part-time and online) may also impact how strict the requirements are or the priority afforded to each requirement. The differences between these modes of study will be covered in more detail in Chapter Four but for now, it's worth bearing in mind that if you're struggling to fully hit every criteria, you might have more chance in being accepted onto courses depending on which mode of study you're looking for and why, with these being aimed at different sub-groups of students.

One way this can be used to your advantage is by using this as an element within your application reasoning to portray a compelling and coherent story, supporting your reasoning for applying to your specific business school. It's worth thinking about which mode of study is likely to fit with your life as well as motivate you the most. An MBA is a sustained commitment and you want to set yourself up for success, reinforcing the conviction that you will succeed and get the most out of the experience throughout your application.

Applications can also include formal scoring mechanisms, particularly if you're applying internationally, as schools look to apply standardised tests to ensure a level of competence at their required level. There are masses of resources available online to help prepare for the test applicable for the universities you're considering but in general, the recommendation is to practise again and again until you're reliably getting the scores you need.

We know that business schools look for candidates with experience and competition for places in some schools is highly competitive, with the bar normally being set higher the more prestigious the university. Some of the below pointers may help you think about what might be unique in your own experience and allow you to build on this, positioning yourself as someone who can bring significant value and who the university should consider as an MBA candidate. Consider not just how you would bring value to the cohort experience, in providing insight on the concepts you will learn from your specific situation, but also in your future position as an alumnus of the university.

- Do you have a unique work history, in your exposure to different industries?
- Do you have history working for industry-leading companies?
- Have you worked in challenging industries (low profit margins, high competition, rapidly changing, highly regulated or even failing companies)?
- Have you both non-profit and for-profit organisational experience?

- Have you worked in both private and public sectors?
- Do you work in an industry that is unique in some way?
- Do you have experience of emerging or innovative technologies?
- Do you have access to key decision makers or are you already a key decision maker yourself?
- Do you work in your own or a family business and want to move your company forward, to realise its full potential?
- Do you have your own business idea that you want to develop and take forward?

Many universities will ask you why you chose that particular institution. This is a really important question and you need to make sure you have a compelling answer. It goes without saying that it needs to be positive about the course and the university! It doesn't need to be complicated, and in fact, keeping it simpler may actually be preferred by some. You can also use this as an opportunity to demonstrate you've done your research and haven't just applied to every university you possibly could on the chance you'd be accepted somewhere (even if this was what you've actually done!).

So, if they have world-renowned teaching or if they have a professor whose interests align with yours or some other unique aspect that they try to showcase, you can work this aspect into your reason. Value for money, the location or method of study fitting with your lifestyle can be perfectly fine reasons and most universities won't be offended if you focus a little on this in your motives. They may even market themselves on this and you should be able to judge this by whether it's mentioned in any of the university endorsed marketing videos or alumni and student interview videos which are often made available. If you're opting for part-time or online study, the fact it can be flexibly worked into your schedule is a large selling factor for the universities, with these increasingly being offered in more and more MBA courses.

Key takeaway points – developing an application:

- Make sure your application evidence is aligned as one coherent and compelling story.
- Cover every requirement criterion as much as you can – give the university no reason to reject you and every reason to welcome you (minimise your negatives and emphasise your positives).
- If you are struggling to meet the criteria, consider if changing your mode of study (full-time, part-time, online) may increase your chances of success. Are more people accepted onto one rather than another? Would the university benefit from having you as a part-time or online student comparatively more than as a full-time student? Is the emphasis the same for the prerequisite criteria on each? What mode of study would motivate you the most and allow you to both contribute and receive the most value?

- Consider not just how you would bring value to the cohort experience, in providing insight on the concepts you will learn from your specific situation, but also in your future position as an alumnus of the university.
- Focus on specific reasons that attract you to that particular MBA course at that particular university.

2.3 Developing your CV/resume

It's worth spending some time looking through good examples of CVs to really refine yours to be the best it can be. There are so many resources available on this online but as a rule, your CV development should be continual and gradual. Try different ways of presenting it to make it more visually appealing. Keep coming back to it with fresh eyes to spot potential errors and ways to improve the language and layout. The more times you do this the better.

As you're looking to potentially do a Masters in Business, your CV needs to be written with this in mind: concise is likely to be received much more favourably than a long, drawn out CV that might be more associated with scientific or academic roles. Your CV should be one or two pages, but no more than two, making sure the space on the page is used fully. As a general rule, you should include the below sections. Specific pointers are included under each one which are detailed here following some great advice from career coaches. Everything can always be improved but by following this as a general guide, it should stand you in good stead. Over the years, I have received countless positive comments from recruiters and employers alike on how well structured my CV has been, through using the below method. If you have access to any career advice services or are able to ask your HR department, an experienced recruitment professional taking a second look at your CV can really help highlight areas of improvement.

- <u>Name</u>
- Keep it professional and simple – there's no need for fancy fonts or overly large text.

- <u>Contact details</u>
- You don't need to include (and potentially shouldn't include due to risk of discrimination, which is often illegal, but can occur subconsciously) date of birth, gender or a photo.
- Stick to the basics to save room on the page: telephone, email and address.
- Email addresses should be professional and to the point, such as just your name. You should make a new, dedicated email if you need to replace any unsuitable current addresses. The more visually appealing you can make this, the better. For example, try to reduce the amount of numbers involved if your name is already taken.

- **Personal statement**
  - Tailor this section to your application: name the university, call out what value you're bringing and why you want to secure a place on the MBA course you're applying for.
  - Lay out your credibility and any applicable transferable skills you have.
  - Highlight a couple of key achievements or experience which may support your application. What are you motivated by? What can you bring? Think about how this supports your application and why you are applying to that specific course ran by that specific university.

- **Education history**
  - Summarise any really old qualifications, rather than going into detail. It might sound obvious, but people don't need to know what you got in Maths in high school at this point! Summarising will also help free up space on the page for more value-adding statements.
  - If there's anything special about anywhere you attended or you had any awards worth mentioning, it's good to bring these to light. For example, your university could have been or may still be one of the top universities for your subject. If it did come or now comes high in rankings, this is definitely worth mentioning, including which rankings it came high in. If the university is accredited by professional bodies and this places them in a unique position or provides credibility,

this will be worth adding. If you really can't think of anything, it's okay to stick to the fundamentals in the education section and we can try a similar approach in the work experience section.

- Work experience
- Make sure your most recent experience is at the top. You generally want more depth provided on the more recent, with gradually less depth and examples provided the further back in your work experience history you go.
- If you worked for any companies or organisations which people may not have heard of, use a couple of lines to provide some key facts and selling points – you might want to include revenue, employees, mission statement and what the business or organisation does. The more you can use this to position the company or organisation in a positive light, the more favourably it will come across on you having been an employee there, particularly if the company isn't very well known. Doing this can also be used to provide context and frame the impact of your achievements.
- When presenting your experience, there are a few techniques out there which you can adopt. Generally, you want to use the present tense for your current position and past tense for previous positions.
- Bullet points are an important tool to break up the text and make it easier to read. A good way to organise these under each of your previous

employers or experience (jobs, businesses, volunteering, or however else might make sense to categorise these) is to use a technique such as the STAR technique:

- o Situation
  The context for your point. What was the challenge?
- o Task
  What was your role in overcoming the challenge?
- o Action
  What did you do to overcome it and how?
- o Result
  This should be quantifiable and ideally communicated through some form of metric or financial gain but can also include softer results.

- Going one step further than STAR, in an even more concise technique is the below approach, which is highly recommended for maximum impact:

1. Role
Start with a powerful active verb, which can be preceded by an adverb if it fits.
   - o *Example: actively led, proactively delivered, or successfully overcame.*

You can then progress into a description of the situation.

- Example: *actively led a team of twenty high-calibre managers through a sustained change initiative.*
2. <u>How</u>

   Now move onto how you achieved what you did. This might speak to how the challenge was complex, required competency, capabilities, took time or was of great scale. You want to identify why you're proud of this achievement and help the reader understand what it took to achieve.
   - Example: *actively led a team of twenty high-calibre managers through a sustained change initiative. Leveraged team strengths to negotiate an incremental change effort, overcoming initial pushback from external stakeholders.*
3. <u>Result</u>

   Once you've specified how challenging this achievement was and why, move into the result.
   - Example: *actively led a team of twenty high-calibre managers through a sustained change initiative. Leveraged team strengths to negotiate an incremental change effort, overcoming initial pushback from external stakeholders, resulting in year on year savings of $2m.*

We can also add a final twist to this to give it even more content and impact by including your learning.

4. Learning
   At the end of sharing the result, share what you took from the experience and how you used the learning to improve yourself or your approach. This level of reflection is a positive trait and shows your adaptability and self-awareness.
   - *Example: my learning from this experience reinforced my belief that an essential part of leading high-calibre teams lies in playing to each individual's strengths.*

All in all, the four sections should be no more than around four or five lines and be as concise as possible. If you're struggling for space on your CV, you can cut the learning section out and add this to the cover letter, using the learning to speak to your development, by linking this into areas you feel you have strengths in already or want to further develop through the MBA.

- <u>Hobbies and interests</u>
- This section should highlight any activities you're involved in outside of work and although it can have many purposes, it's often used to show you're a normal human being that can have fun too and aren't just about work! Many people are often tempted to exaggerate on this section but it's worth being honest as it can be a section that

can attract questions, particularly if there are more unusual activities mentioned.
- Apart from a rapport builder, you can use this section to demonstrate any other activities you're doing which might show further transferable skills, as well as displaying commitment and passion for your interests. This can easily be used to translate well into the overall view of your application by showing a level of enthusiasm that will likely spill over into your MBA experience.

So now we have been through the main sections, we can consider some general points. You can use the order of the education and work experience sections to prioritise your strengths, bringing whatever you're more confident with to the top. The halo effect is a well-known cognitive bias phenomenon that can be used to your advantage in recruitment and CV writing. The theory surmises that a positive perception in one area will have a halo effect, resulting in a higher chance of perceiving other areas in a positive light. You can use this bias to your advantage by trying to present as many positives as possible, in the most favourable way possible, ideally starting with the best.

As a side note, make sure your spelling and grammar are 100% correct. This may be obvious but can't be stressed enough. A couple of errors may be overlooked in an MBA application if the rest of your application is great but for something so small, it's frankly not worth the risk. Plus, getting it 100% right is a good habit to get into for subsequent job applications, which will often automatically discount anyone with errors. I would advise asking a trusted and appropriately diligent and competent friend, colleague, or family member to proof-read your application as our minds become accustomed to what we write and can easily miss mistakes that might otherwise be quite obvious.

Key takeaway points – developing your CV/resume:

- Invest the time refining your CV to be the best it can be in both content and structure. This will not only help you pre-MBA but during the MBA and also following the MBA in your likely job search.
- Keep coming back to your CV with fresh eyes to minimise the chance of errors and incrementally improve content, visual appeal and structure.
- Focus each section and use the four-step approach for maximum impact in outlining your work experience.
- Use the halo effect to your advantage.
- Make sure your spelling and grammar are 100% correct. A trusted, competent and diligent friend, colleague or family member may be willing to help.

2.4 Employer references

Securing strong and positive references can be really difficult depending on your employment situation and you'll need to play it carefully if you see any potential risks. The perception your employer has of you doing an MBA can heavily influence when you start a potential journey to applying for an MBA, due to references usually being a required element of the application process. This gives your employer some degree of power unless you have other options for gaining employment references.

You may be really lucky and your employer might be fully supportive of you doing an MBA, recognising it as your ambition to develop yourself and the potential for it to enable you to add more value to your employer. However, MBAs can represent fast-track progression so if, for example, you work in a small company and there isn't much room for progression, they may see you upskilling as a threat to them losing you as an employee in your inevitable and potentially now fast-approaching search for a pay-rise or promotion. There could also be concerns about your workload and ability to balance the needs of the business with what will be a serious time commitment to complete the MBA if you're opting for part time or online courses. If you're opting for a full-time course, there may be considerations on how best to cover your role with added uncertainty on whether you will return.

A less-supportive manager may delay giving you a reference and exercise control in this way. A range of reasons might be provided for this, whether it's they don't feel you're ready yet, positioning it as part of a series of development stages or offering alternative company training courses (remember the myth: there are other ways of replicating the business school and MBA knowledge and experience). This can be as a result of personal perceptions, as we covered earlier, due to culture within your company or may result from worries around setting precedents of supporting future employees financially or through needing to provide time to study. However, in many cases it's also worth not assuming any initial resistance is malicious. Any resistance can be a useful prompt for self-reflection and a chance to seek support from your manager in developing an action plan to help you get to where you need to be from their perspective.

As a first step, it's worth trying to gauge what your line manager's and employer's positions may be on MBAs. To achieve this, it could be positioned as something you were thinking about and wondered if there might be any options for you to explore it further with their support. Approaching this in a soft way, asking for support and exploring what might be possible to help you develop, is much more likely to receive a positive response as an initial step rather than stating you'll be leaving to do a full-time MBA and that you want their support. Your ability to involve your line manager and employer in the decision and your development path is a pivotal way in gaining their support – you need to bring them along with you.

Once you have this initial feel on the level of support you're likely to receive, an open conversation to understand the motives behind any pushback is key to you overcoming any resistance. For example, if your boss is resistant because of the worry of having to fund you through the course, offering to amend your contract to be tied into continuing to work for your existing company for a set number of years post-graduation may be an option. Alternatively, you may even want to commit to funding the MBA yourself. Many of the roles recruiting recent MBA graduates can be willing to pay off your debt to your previous employer as part of gaining you as an employee, but this would need to be negotiated as part of any post-MBA job search and can't always be relied on.

Remember to be clear on why you want to pursue an MBA and the value it will bring to both you personally whilst also focusing on how it will benefit the company. This should help alleviate concerns around you developing yourself and then moving on, through reiterating your commitment to your company. The more you can quantify the benefits into actual gains or advancements for the company, the better. For example, can you demonstrate how you pursuing an MBA can help you to more effectively deliver or improve on the business development or sales goals within your company or other long-term strategic project or challenge? If you can, it's worth going into any conversations with these details to hand, to help support your request.

If the resistance to providing a reference continues, you may have a few other options still available and will need to carefully consider your best path forward. Assuming you left on good terms, one option might be to ask a previous employer, depending on how long it's been since you worked there and whether the application process allows for this. This might be easily explainable to the university if asked but you should have a reasonable answer ready just in case if you choose to go down this route. Having difficulties securing an employer reference from your current employer does happen so it is likely the university may be able to be somewhat flexible on this. Depending on the process and language used in this part of the application, you may need to clarify the requirements with the admissions department if getting an employer reference from your current employer may be difficult.

Another possibility within this scenario to be aware of is not alienating your current employer or boss in the unlikely but possible event where they decline to provide a reference for you and then find out you've sourced one from elsewhere and are starting an MBA anyway. This might not be an issue if you're choosing to go down a full-time MBA route and aren't planning on returning to the company but may turn into an issue if you're looking to study via an online, distance-learning route and need to continue working there.

Getting your current employer's full buy-in is obviously essential in any part-time study route as these often require attendance during what would traditionally be work time, needing your employer to commit to some sort of flexible working arrangement. If your request is initially declined by your current employer, continuing to raise your wish for support with your employer over time in development reviews or one-to-one meetings with your manager is also an option. However, this may take time to overcome any resistance and may create some annoyance if continued for some less cooperative or understanding managers.

Another option may be to seek a reference from other activities you might do in your spare time, particularly if these are of an entrepreneurial nature. These will naturally greatly vary from person to person but may be something you can explore if the application requirements and business school allows for it. You might for example also hold a position in a charity or run a small side business from which you may have a network of business relationships you could rely on, such as a key supplier or buyer. As well as these likely more recent options, if you have studied for an undergraduate degree in the past, an academic reference may provide another alternative. However, in exploring this option it's worth considering just how long ago this was and if there are any more recent options you can explore that may provide a stronger, more professional view of your character.

In asking your employer for a reference, it's also worth considering who in your organisation you should ask. If resistance is coming or could come from your line manager, are there others you could ask? Do you have a mentor, or could you seek one out, with the intention of asking them for their reference in the future? Once you have identified someone you could call on, consider the quality of recommendation you're likely to receive. Can you trust that they'll give you a good reference and give you the support you need? Is there any chance of them being overly critical? Have you already spoken with them about you taking the opportunity and how did they react? If you ask anyone other than your line manager, is there a way you can do this without alienating your current line manager and putting the other person in a difficult position?

It's worth exploring this a little with those you're considering asking before asking them to help support you. Some universities allow recommendations to be submitted directly to the university so you may never find out what was said and how it impacted your application. Many forms request details on your development needs, so it is worth aligning with those endorsing your skills and capabilities on what you believe these are, providing any real-world examples from within your business to support your logic. Providing this up front can help ensure your reference aligns with your personal statement and other supporting material in your application.

As part of seeking a reference and the potential bias in the application process from the university, it's also worth considering who the most senior person in your network you can reasonably ask for a recommendation from might be. The more senior this person, on first impressions, the more positively this is likely to reflect on your application. Someone reviewing your application in the business school might be more impressed that you have the CEO, Vice President or Senior Director within your company recommending you for the course and speaking to your abilities than a Team Manager or

Functional Manager. This might not always be realistically possible but is worth considering if you can. It is still worth asking for more senior support wherever you can, not just to hopefully help in providing a more favourably received reference, but also in raising your profile within your company. This will very often make initial connections for you which you can then follow up on and develop through your MBA to increase the chances of you securing greater career opportunities at a later stage.

As well as considering who the most senior person in your network is who you can reasonably ask for a reference from, you should think about the strength of the recommendation you're likely to receive. When requesting this support, it's really important to your chances of success that you impress on whoever is endorsing you that their input is likely to play a fundamental role in the overall success of the application. Depending on how well the person you're asking knows you and your work, it may help to provide evidence for them of the traits and successes you would like them to highlight. Being specific with them about what the university is looking for in candidates will help to align them with what you need them to say and help you achieve as strong a reference as you can.

You will likely find out through this part of the application process where you stand with your employer and this can lead to some eye-opening results, which can come back down to the reputation MBAs have and how this is perceived by others. Don't let this put you off taking a long-term view with your ambitions. If your research suggests an MBA will help you to achieve your goals, then it is worth continuing to explore as a potential option and it's worth exploring this with the support of your employer initially. If this support isn't forthcoming, it is worth taking the time to fully understand why. Where the stakes of you continuing to hold a job may be high, job security may rank higher on your priorities than trying to push your employer into supporting you to complete an MBA. A softer approach is usually better, but it may mean you need to go down the self-funding online route and supporting yourself if you believe it may help you in the future. Where job security is crucial for you and alternative jobs may be limited, your employer may exercise their comparatively greater power over your decision, but you still have options you can explore. It might take you comparatively more time, but pursuing an MBA is often still possible. You do have the option of pursuing an MBA independent of an employer.

Within my cohort there was a real mix of stories around the employer support people received. Several had to go it on their own once their employers had refused time off, financial support or flexibility in working. Yet many did get the full support of their employer, with several allowing time off to study full-time with a guaranteed job when they returned. However the situation plays out for you, the support you get will speak volumes for the company and whether they truly believe in supporting and developing their employees. Once you get over the hurdle of securing good employer references, you'll be free to continue to make your choice of whether they're the employer you want to continue to work for both during and following the MBA.

Key takeaway points – employer references:

- Be clear on your commitment to your employer and the benefit to them of you studying for an MBA - try to be tangible in what it will bring.
- Assess the likely support you'll receive in asking for references in the context of your options for different modes of study.
- Understand the motives behind any pushback to identify how you might best overcome this.
- Identify the best and most senior potential providers of references. Explore the idea with them before asking in order to help bring them along with you on the decision.
- Consider the quality of reference you're likely to receive from those you've identified, ensuring you are comfortable those you ask will provide a favourable recommendation.
- Seek to secure as strong a reference as possible. Share what universities look for in candidates with those providing endorsement, as well as any examples of your work to help guide those supporting you in providing the most favourable recommendation possible.
- Share your development needs with those providing a reference to ensure alignment with

your application, backing these up with examples to support your reasoning.

2.5 Bias in the process

We've talked a bit about positive bias generally in the process, but there is a range of bias which could occur in the application process as a whole and you'll need to do some investigating to see if you may be able to play to your strengths in any areas of opportunity. Bias is still found in business and academic settings and it's worth at least being aware of where it could come into play for your individual circumstances, in the context of the business schools you may be applying to. Being aware of where bias may be present can help you to address and overcome it.

Increasingly more is being done in businesses and academia alike to tackle discrimination and unfair bias. Whether it's to do with gender, race or any number of a range of potential areas, it's right that universities play a part in evening the playing field for under-represented groups. With this being said, despite global diversity in many MBA courses, gender representations remain imbalanced with business schools often still having a high proportion of male candidates. Within my own cohort, around 70% of those attending in-person classes were male. These were attended by those studying online, part-time and full-time together as one group, with in-person attendance optional on the online and part-time courses. Most organisations continue to push towards gender equality and balance and if you're applying to a feeder school of traditionally male dominated industries, this may be a consideration in the university admissions criteria to encourage diversity. However, the presence and effectiveness of these diversity targets will vary by university and industry. By being aware of the current and target levels of diversity in your academic and industry setting, this can allow you to understand where bias may still exist, allowing you to challenge the norm and play to your strengths.

Some universities can be located in quite deprived rural regions and business schools often have strong links with local businesses. This can count in your favour if you're from the local area, both from a convenience point of view and the university often wanting to support the development of the local region. This symbiotic relationship is a strong motivator for some universities who are genuinely invested in improving their locality. This is likely to be as a result of the personal motivations of the staff influencing the organisational attitude towards this – it's perfectly understandable for the staff, many of who will live and work in the area, to have a natural affiliation with the people and businesses there.

More students from the local area provide more opportunities to link with businesses, a stronger collaborative network for applied research and more local opportunities for students, with the further potential for additional future local students. You might find that even in MBAs advertised as international, there will be a strong local cohort presence. This is really beneficial if you're applying from that locality as your network will both have a strong local element to it whilst also having international presence. As an additional benefit post-MBA, you're also excellently poised to maintain strong relationships with those physically closer to you. However, if you're looking to maximise global exposure, it is worth investigating this aspect to understand if a university with more local affiliations will provide what you are seeking.

You have an opportunity to create a positive first impression by networking with the staff ahead of submitting your application and establishing contacts within the business school. You can explore this in a variety of ways depending on your situation, whether it's finding out more about what research the business school is conducting in an area you're currently focusing on in work or discussing the application process and your suitability with those running the course. Assuming you can make a good impression in these interactions, you can include your growing network into your application as part of your motivation to applying to that business school in particular. By taking action, this will demonstrate a strong commitment to the school and your personal development and be a good indicator you would continue such activities once accepted. Aside from the benefits of creating a positive first impression, gaining the insights provided by this networking on the characteristics and culture of the business school can be a crucial part of the process in understanding if you do indeed want to pursue a place on that specific MBA course.

Key takeaway points – bias in the process:

- Being aware of where bias may be present can help you to address and overcome it, by challenging the norm and playing to your strengths.
- Consider if there may be locational bias in the universities application process and if this is likely to influence the success of your application and the characteristics of your future network. Understand the MBA cohort international and local representation and whether a strong local representation is something you would value, if this is something that characterises the MBA cohort at that particular university.
- Consider networking with the business school staff and establishing connections with the school prior to applying, which you can use to make a good first impression and demonstrate your commitment. This will also provide a network you could begin to call on in your everyday work through the many areas academia interacts with industry.
- Use the opportunity of networking with business school staff to understand as much as possible around the characteristics and culture of the business school, ensuring that you gain the insights you need to be sure you want to pursue a place on that specific MBA course.

Chapter Three

The MBA Demographic, Networking and Reputation

3.1 The MBA demographic

MBA courses attract people with ambition and those wanting to improve themselves. This in itself can lead to a noticeably generally positive, explorative culture. You'll notice definite categories of people within a typical cohort, with each having distinct motives and priorities. Business schools often publish their demographic information, including gender ratio, average age, nationalities and industry and you can use this to compare potential business schools to get a feel for how international and how diverse the cohorts generally are. International diversity can present great opportunities to demonstrate your ability to work in global teams, with this being a really positive skill that many multinational corporations and global businesses look for in candidates. Similarly, some business schools act as feeder universities to certain industries or attract students from specific professions, with many universities doing this through partnerships with key organisations. Clearly, if you want to move into an industry associated with the university, this might make the potential networking opportunities much more appealing at one business school over another.

Discovering the differing motives and priorities in others can be one of the most insightful aspects of networking. Through this, you will gain a deep understanding behind the reasons your cohort will act the way they do and have the viewpoints they hold throughout your interactions on the course. As you would expect, there are usually plenty of ambitious and mobile professionals in their mid to late twenties and early thirties, which usually make up a reasonable amount of any MBA class. Their motives can range from simply upskilling and climbing the corporate ladder to changing careers and targeting highly sought-after industries or roles. These are also some of the most valuable students within the cohort to network with if you're looking for potential opportunities to progress your own career and income. This is because, generally, this group are more likely to be at an earlier stage in their career and may be more willing to grow their network and maintain meaningful connections to support their own development, with sharing opportunities and insights being a part of this.

In the next category, are those with young families, who may be a little less mobile but still often pursuing upskilling and career progression. It's common for people in this category to be company sponsored and they also often attend as part of their professional development, with some doing the MBA as part of company requirements for upskilling, on the path to more senior leadership roles. For these professionals, ambition can vary. This is because, if they hadn't pursued the MBA as part of their own personal goals and aren't funding it from their own pocket, they can be slightly less invested and have reduced risk associated with getting comparatively fewer benefits from the process. In essence, they are more likely to do the minimum to get by and may readily prioritise other areas of their life. This is obviously fine and completely understandable, just something to be aware of when networking. This group of students may be less likely to change industry and so may be a more reliable contact if their industry or role is an area you're interested in, or if similarities or contrasts may exist with your own work which may make for interesting and productive interactions.

There is also another distinct, but much smaller category which includes very highly experienced and very senior professionals. These students may have been strongly encouraged or even practically forced into doing the MBA by their employer in order to secure their next natural role, or alternatively may be pursuing the MBA as part of a self-development journey. Students in this category are often fascinating and much more willing to be frank and open, as they have less to lose or gain and often might see the MBA as a bit of fun. You might unsurprisingly find maintaining a meaningful or beneficial connection with these professionals to be difficult post-MBA, depending on their personality and attitude toward networking. However, if you do manage to form a good connection, these contacts can be really great sounding boards. The difficulty here is being able to offer them something in return over the long-term if you can't rely on friendship alone or some other sort of reciprocal professional relationship.

Demographics vary by course type, with the executive MBAs targeting more established professionals. However, if you can get on an executive MBA and are looking for higher-level contacts, this can be a really good way of developing these connections. The downside to executive MBAs in this regard is the cohorts are usually smaller and as a result there is less chance of someone already being in an industry you want to build contacts in, if this is one of your hopes. Therefore, although the quantity of potential business relationships may be fewer, any you do make are almost certain to be of higher quality, with more chance of you making and keeping more meaningful and long-term connections.

Depending on your priorities and career aspirations, it may be worth holding off on starting an MBA for a few more additional years and pursuing an executive MBA course instead. However, it's worth doing a lot more investigating on the types of people being enrolled onto these courses as universities are likely to be a lot more selective in order to maintain their reputation and the calibre of students (think a magnified version of the positive application bias). As part of this bias, you will more than likely need to demonstrate competence in a senior role to gain a place on one of these courses and the level of seniority required varies by university.

Part-time and online MBAs tend to have higher proportions of people trying to juggle multiple commitments. They also generally come with a lower price tag which can make them slightly easier to afford, or at least represent better value. Depending on the university, for some of the business schools who offer a good reputation whilst not being in the traditionally super-elite category, this can offer anywhere between a 10% and around a 40% discount to the full-time fees in tuition alone. This comparatively better value for money, potentially running into low five figure sums worth of saving, can result in higher proportions of self-funded students in the cohort who maintain full or part-time employment whilst studying. This can make for some very practically focused, real-time contacts who may be able to help with job searches and applications as well as contributing more current experiences to the cohort's discussions. As many within this situation will end up changing industry both during and after the course, you may develop a greater understanding of the background experience and extended network of your cohort than you otherwise would within another mode of study.

The most commonly attended MBA course type firmly remains the full-time MBA, with these offering a cohort who can afford to take a year or two out of work. This can result in some wealthy and well-connected contacts who may be self-funding, those who have taken a lot of personal risk to be there as well as a few who will likely be funded by their employer and are fortunate enough for their employer to be willing to support them by holding a role for their return. As a result, the full-time MBA can have a very motivated cohort as the stakes are much higher, which can result in increased competitiveness within assessed interactions and opportunities following the MBA. As well as this being the most attended type of course, many universities only offer this as a study option, with this potentially forcing students who want to attend that specific school into choosing the full-time mode of study.

The demographic on the MBA courses is likely to hold different value to you depending on your own reasons for pursuing an MBA but it's worth thinking about whether this matters for you in the context of your available options. If making connections in your chosen industry or field is key to progressing and this is supported by the feedback you've gained when researching how best to progress in your situation, then it's worth looking for courses that can offer this. However, if you're looking to improve your general business acumen and are open to a wide range of opportunities, a more diverse network could be beneficial and you may want to consider courses with generally broader cohorts. Although you're naturally less likely to connect with those in your network who don't share your values and are less likely to make meaningful long-term business relationships as a result, being aware of this and going into the experience with your eyes open to this potential personal bias is an advantage. This isn't about excluding people from your network, but about understanding where mutually beneficial relationships aligned with your values may exist. Similarly, it may be worthwhile pushing yourself to go against your personal bias and develop relationships with those who do contrast with your values. It is these people that often provide you with an alternative view, which can be worthwhile in challenging your own assumptions.

Key takeaway points – the MBA demographic:

- Take the time to consider the motives and priorities of those likely to be in your cohort – are they aligned to what you're looking for and what you're looking to achieve?
- Once you're on an MBA course, understand the impact that differing priorities will have on the actions and viewpoints of your cohort, whilst also considering the potential value of your future connections to your network.
- A lot of the value coming from the MBA originates from the experience of the cohort. Similarly, diversity is key to success in organisations. Building your network to include this diversity of backgrounds and views can be a great way to challenge your own assumptions.

3.2 Networking internally versus externally

We know a lot of attention is given to networking on MBA courses and this falls into the category of networking externally to your own organisation. This is key for certain industries and roles in building contacts and being able to work with others, supported through building understanding of their differing perspectives and industries. This not only strengthens your wider business acumen but can also offer new insights which you can apply to your own industry. This can be through your knowledge of similar challenges which may be being overcome elsewhere under different guises, or through the use of different techniques being used elsewhere for similar issues to those which you may be facing.

However, throughout your journey you may need to weigh the importance of external networking against the value of networking internally, within your own organisation – especially if you're limited on time. This is a fundamental part of the MBA Blueprint for Success – it's great if you develop an extensive and high-value network outside of your own company, but if you're hoping to stay and progress at your current company, ask for an increase in salary after the course finishes or even pursue roles in the same industry, it's vital that you don't neglect your internal network. You need a good balance of both and although you may want to focus on one more than the other depending on the situation, you definitely want to make sure that you don't completely neglect one or the other. You never know what opportunities you will inadvertently be closing yourself off to.

Although this book considers your internal network as being your current employer throughout the MBA, if you're pursuing a full-time MBA you may have left an employer to complete the course. From this perspective, if you would be open to going back to your previous employer, it's worth keeping in touch with them through the experiences you're having on the course. Alternatively, if you have specific desired future employers in mind, you can use this perspective of internal versus external networking as internal being the companies you may want to work at in the future. By targeting these to try and involve in your MBA work, you also gain the added benefit of building your network in these companies before and during any potential job search.

This brings us back to the perception value offered by MBAs. The perceptions of your colleagues and superiors need to be carefully managed as much as possible in your own current or future potential company, which can be supported through your networking. If there are a lot of people already holding MBAs, your ability to build a positive perception of your skills and capabilities through networking may be slightly easier as others will understand the topics you're learning and the value they bring. As part of helping to further improve this perception and your reputation, you should be trying to demonstrate to your manager, senior leaders and internal network how it's bringing value to your everyday work and trying to apply the tools and concepts you're learning wherever you can and wherever it makes sense to.

Most MBA courses will guide you on how to effectively manage change and it might not be immediately obvious you're applying concepts from the MBA. It's worth highlighting this link to your line manager and those who may need to see the connection to realise the value the MBA is bringing to you and to the business. Demonstrating this value is key if you're going to maximise your opportunities and increase your income as you'll more than likely need evidence of this added value to add justification to your case. The wider you share this benefit where it makes sense to within your internal network, the better. The more you can quantify the added value you've been able to bring, in financial or other measurable gains, the more likely it is you will receive a favourable outcome in using this as a way to justify your request for higher pay in any end of year review or new job negotiation.

<u>Key takeaway points – networking internally versus externally:</u>

- Balance is needed in developing your internal and external networks – your internal network may actually be more important to maximising your potential career opportunities.
- Manage perceptions in your own current or potential future organisation by demonstrating the value the MBA is bringing to you and the business, making this link clear and the benefit quantifiable. This will support future conversations around career progression, increasing your income or securing future employment if you're using your work as an opportunity to expand your network and identify new opportunities.

3.3 Internal versus external professional reputation

In this section, we will analyse some of the different stakeholders who you may need to consider when developing and maintaining your professional reputation in relation to your MBA. It's worth thinking about how you can and should interact with these people throughout your MBA journey to maximise the potential opportunities available to you in your situation. This isn't about taking advantage of people, but what you may be able to offer others and what they may be able to offer you in return. You will generally find that most people are more than willing to help you – you often just need to ask in the right way.

We mentioned at the start of the book that having an MBA often carries an elite status and that this can fairly or unfairly open doors for you. The way this is achieved is through managing your reputation and making the hype of having an MBA work for you whilst showcasing your skills and capabilities. Through effectively managing your reputation in your internal and external network, you can unlock the doors that might have otherwise been locked. However, the key is in exploring where those opportunities, or doors, actually are and putting in the time to pursuing them. There are plenty of doors out there, but you have to be willing to explore where they are – you can do this through a combination of networking, building your reputation and acting on opportunities.

Internal reputation

- <u>Employer/line management</u>

If there aren't many others in your management team holding an MBA, this can have both positive and negative consequences for your reputation development. On the plus side, you will stand out and may have more of a halo effect than if there were many others with this experience. On the downside, this may stir up negative emotions in some which you might want to try and overcome. Faced with this challenge, you will likely have to work harder to prove the value and the benefit the MBA is bringing to you and the organisation. The negative emotions can vary significantly from person to person but can be based in jealousy, resentment, or thoughts around you wasting your own or the company's time. Whatever the reasoning, it's important you try to overcome this as early as possible and are consistent with your efforts. It's important for your future career that you seek out and deliberately share relevant benefits as part of your work with senior leaders in your network.

Approaching this in the right way is key, so make sure to take a soft approach and make sure you've thought about the potential outcomes extensively before making a move. Weigh up the motivations of those you're trying to sell this value to and be clear on what you're asking for and why you're sharing this with them. For example, are you asking for an endorsement on your proposal for change? Is it an exercise around informing them on great work that has already been done? Or are you asking for their input on your work and whether they have any constructive feedback? If you're lucky enough to have a supportive manager, involving them in this is a great way to expand your potential of getting a promotion or increasing your income during or following your MBA, by having them act as an advocate for the benefit you're bringing and your increased capabilities.

During assignments for your MBA, you often have the opportunity to look at a specific business problem or business of your choice, applying theories and tools from your course to that situation and recommending ways to improve. This can be a fantastic opportunity to tailor your assessed work to the role or organisation you're looking to move in to and you can share this work both whilst you're writing it up and afterwards. This can be especially powerful if you use it as an opportunity to try and bring real value to your company or another company at the same time as fulfilling your MBA assignment requirements. This can add more pressure to you whilst you're in the middle of the MBA but is a great way of trying to unlock higher marks by demonstrating you're bringing real value to real businesses through doing the work, which often goes above and beyond assessment requirements. From an internal network and reputation perspective, tailoring your assignments can demonstrate the value you're bringing in real-time during your MBA. In turn, this can increase how visible you are to your senior leaders whilst allowing you to use the opportunity to gain their insights on the topics you're writing about – another win-win scenario in your MBA journey.

As with the considerations on networking, if you're attending a full-time course, reputation building should be pursued both within your existing or previous company, as well as companies you are potentially targeting to move into if that's your intention. Continuing to build on your reputation in previous companies, where this makes sense, is still worthwhile as they already know you. This can be a blessing or a curse depending on the company and the perception they have of you, which is why this needs to be managed well if you are to explore this as an option.

Where potential hiring managers from a previous company know your prior capabilities, they may struggle to realise just how much additional ability you will gain from an MBA and it will be up to you to share experiences with them to demonstrate this. Conversely, if this perception is managed well, this can be really beneficial for both parties – you already know the company and they already know you would fit as an employee, by the nature of you having worked there before. This familiarity can make securing a more senior role with them comparatively easier than if you were to be going through a selection process with a completely new company. However, this potential opportunity is situation dependent as it assumes you left on good terms.

For employers who are sponsoring you in part or full tuition or supporting you through other means, it's important to remember their vested interest in your success. The support you have been provided will likely have been signed off and endorsed by at least one other person depending on the size of the company and you shouldn't forget about keeping these advocates on-side. Depending on their role and interest, this can be from as simple as just sharing some of your work from the MBA and sharing how you're doing to getting their input on certain aspects of your work or topics you're exploring on the course. The fact that they endorsed you will likely mean they are keen to see you be successful and so should be happy to hear feedback of how you're doing, confirming they made the right decision. As you begin to share more, discuss more concepts and how you may be able to bring them into the company, they will begin to appreciate your uplift in capability, which can help your case for translating this into higher pay and promotion opportunities.

There may actually be an expectation for you to be delivering improvements resulting from your work on your MBA. You may have sold the benefits of you doing an MBA to your company on this basis, or it may be a perception that has formed within your management team on this being what an MBA represents. In this situation, you would essentially be forced into sharing your work and this may form a more formal process. Without doing this, your reputation may suffer and your status benefit of having an MBA may also reduce so it is important you're aware of the expectations of your employer from the outset to make sure you're aligned. This may already be apparent from your application process but either way, it's worth checking in with your line manager on what their expectations are of you both during and following the course.

- Colleagues

Many of the reputation considerations which apply to your line manager and management team also apply to colleagues. Although not everyone will be seeking to get an MBA to drive change and improvement within businesses, the vast majority are, and this will often be the expectation of others on what an MBA graduate can deliver. Whilst your manager usually has the authority to approve or reject development ideas you may have from their position in the organisation, colleagues can often heavily influence the success of your ideas and work, through their willing support and engagement or lack of it.

Many MBA courses explore the challenge of gaining willing cooperation from teams when undergoing change initiatives and there is a wide range of material available on the subject. This often spans across MBA subjects, not just impacting and being impacted by change management and technology adoption, but also being heavily influenced through leadership and management styles as well as organisational culture. From a personal perspective, your ability to initially lead change and improvement may come down to how and where you fit within the team as well as your prior reputation within the team before starting the MBA. Although change and improvement are never impossible, the degree of difficulty you may experience will likely vary considerably and it is this difficulty which can be increased or reduced through your professional reputation.

As we covered at the start of this book, colleagues can be polarised on the subject of MBAs and you may be surprised by the reactions and subtle resistance of those on your team to any new ideas you may have if they are framed as coming from your MBA course. This resistance can often be quite personal as they may feel threatened by their perception of your career trajectory or feel as though you're gaining an unfair advantage over them if they know the company has supported you on your journey through the MBA. Whatever their reasoning, subconscious or conscious, you have an opportunity from the beginning of your journey to try to bring as many people on your side as possible.

As with your line manager and management team, your approach is going to play a fundamental part in increasing the likelihood of successfully gaining the support of your colleagues. One distinctive difference in approach which can have a huge impact in how you are perceived is how you are broaching the subject you're looking to raise with others. For example, if you are wanting to explore a change in a strategy and this would need the buy-in of colleagues, going to them with a finished idea of how this would work in practice could cause them to resist the idea from the outset. You haven't involved your colleagues in the idea's conception, they have no background to your thought process and the intention and benefits of the change in strategy might not be clear.

Instead, to overcome this potential resistance, you could explore the idea with the team initially, asking for constructive feedback and for input on any aspects which you may not have thought of. Simply by asking the team for feedback and incorporating this, they become invested in the solution and are more likely to be supportive. It will also give you a chance to hear any of their concerns from an early stage, allowing you to overcome these or design your change in such a way that it does not trigger this apprehension, where it may otherwise prevent you from proceeding any further. Similarly, if your proposed change affects a large team, sharing with a couple of the team first may help you gain key supporters to help you share further. This can also be a useful tactic in getting the potentially most opposed colleagues on-side first, by pairing them with colleagues most likely to be supportive. You can then actively work within this smaller sub-team to try and overcome any potential resistance at an early stage.

Obviously, this is just an example and the complexity of proposed change initiatives can cause complicated organisational and personal challenges but there are also many other ways of overcoming these challenges you can explore. By being open to trying different approaches in engaging with your colleagues, you can ensure your reputation with your co-workers is the most favourable it can be, further supporting the likelihood of you securing favourable future opportunities. By keeping the team in support of your work, demonstrating the value it could also bring to them, you ensure they will remain open to new ideas, which will in turn help you prove the value your MBA is bringing to you and your company.

- <u>Wider internal network</u>

It can be worth considering how you can manage and build your reputation throughout your MBA journey with your wider internal network, who may provide another important source of potential opportunities. This could be family or friends who might also double up as professional connections, putting you in touch with others who may have opportunities, or you may have other acquaintances through hobbies or interests. For example, you might be involved in charity work, societies, or sports, providing a natural extended network as a non-standard route to further potential opportunities.

As this aspect of your internal network is clearly not about your professional advancement, this likely won't be (and probably shouldn't be) on the forefront of your mind when you're with these individuals. However, as you'll naturally already be spending time with these people and sharing the fact that you're doing an MBA, it just might be worth bearing in mind if a conversation about careers and potential work might be worthwhile.

You may find that when you share the fact that you're doing an MBA, others are interested in your experience and journey as they begin to consider something similar for themselves. This can be a great way to share your experiences and help others in finding their way. My own experience of this is part of the reason behind why this book was written – many people rightly consider MBAs as an option to upskill and progress their careers and if you or I are able to help people to find their way in a similar situation to where we once found ourselves, we should do what we can.

External reputation

- ### Prospective employers

Your reputation amongst prospective employers can be crucial in securing a role post-graduation. Particularly if you're on a full-time MBA, the university should be supporting you in exploring your opportunities, but you will have to do the work to find suitable prospective employers and manage your reputation once you begin interacting with them. Career fairs can be a great way to meet prospective employers and make connections, but you will need to engage with those representatives and others from the companies you're interested in following this initial interaction and begin to build your visibility and reputation with them.

This might begin either leading up to or during your MBA, with the potential to increase your reputation in a similar way to the approach you might take with a current employer. Many of the same potential methods would apply, such as tailoring your assignments to the company and sharing examples of your work, particularly where this may add value for them. By tailoring your assignments to the company you're interested in and sharing key points from this with them for input and feedback, you will be able to increase your visibility whilst also deepening your understanding of the company. This will not only help you in your assignments but will also support you in your application for a role with the company, due to your deeper understanding of the role, organisation and industry.

You will need to research and gauge who specifically might be appropriate to share any relevant work with and be very clear on why you want to share it. It can be a double-edged sword in that if your work or presentation is poor or your reasoning for asking a specific employee isn't right, it may actually hurt your reputation. It is better to try to begin to form relationships before sharing and going into the relationship with too high expectations. Beginning with your interest in the company and the day to day work of your specific contact may be a good start and it is through this that you can gauge whether it might be appropriate or useful to share anything further. LinkedIn and company websites are definitely useful in targeting specific potential contacts and providing the information needed to assess if it might make sense to reach out to them. Just remember to be positive, curious and open to what the interaction may bring.

If you're looking to apply for roles in a particular company, it is far better to apply direct via the company website rather than through recruitment agencies. In addition to applying direct, by reaching out to the recruiting and hiring managers directly, you can make the best impression possible and make them aware of your application. Many recruitment agencies screen candidates even before submitting applications to a company, so by not going through an agency, you skip this artificial screening stage, allowing the company to decide for themselves. A few companies may use nominated recruitment agencies, but this is not a common practice and the majority of companies refuse to accept candidates through agencies as standard practice. Even if you're unsuccessful the first time, your application may still be noticed, allowing you to build some visibility with the company for any subsequent applications.

- MBA network

Before your MBA, you may have the opportunity to connect with your upcoming cohort through LinkedIn, as many applicants update their profiles to reflect their upcoming university details. This is worth a quick look to see if you can connect with your future peers and begin to build a relationship prior to the course starting. It's down to personal preference whether or not you feel this is worthwhile, but it may make the initial networking events slightly less awkward if you know the background to a few people already and will allow you to begin to form a network of people you may be able to call on in the future for support.

During your MBA, your reputation within your cohort network is something that can work to your advantage if you manage to cultivate it well. This may come in particularly useful if you want to talk through concepts or the requirements for assignments and this interaction can lead to higher marks as a result of using other's views to understand the material and requirements to a higher standard. In doing this, you should take care not to share work as this can lead to plagiarism which is very likely to be picked up by the plagiarism software used on written assignments. However, the sharing of ideas and perspectives is something that is encouraged and can be really worthwhile in developing your understanding and knowledge.

Following your MBA, the network you have built during your course will form a set of connections who are most likely to understand the same challenges you may be facing. This understanding can make them more receptive to trying to provide opportunities or advice on the areas you're facing challenges in and it's worth reaching out to those who you feel may be able to support. The extended group of people who have also graduated from your university with an MBA, both prior to and following yours, also provide a network you can reach out to for advice or potential opportunities.

With new graduates every year, your network is continually expanding, so it's worth keeping an eye out for new potential ways to build your reputation in your career and that of your network through new opportunities that may be presented. Your network gained through an MBA can be particularly advantageous to your employer if you're in a role where industry and trend insights may be useful. Your ability to talk things through with others who share the experience of the MBA and your knowledge in the concepts learned can be incredibly valuable in quickly identifying areas of added value to you and your business. Through all of these potential contacts from your MBA experience, you can build and maintain your reputation with other stakeholders within your network.

- Industry network

Your current or desired industry will have networks that exist through organisational connections and groups. There are lots of ways to explore these and they can be a great way of building your reputation and extending your network in the process. To find these networks, LinkedIn is a good place to start. If you engage with any of the topics in the network group, this can appear in the news feeds of your connections depending on the group privacy settings and whether any of your existing LinkedIn connections are also in that group. This can increase your visibility to those who you work with or are looking to work with and may help you get your ideas and work noticed more.

Within organisations, there are often formal and informal networks which can sometimes exist between competitors or complementary industries. These can be fascinating groups to be a part of and will help support you in gaining a much deeper understanding of industry challenges and opportunities. Due to their nature, they may not be very visible and depending on those involved in them and their formality, may require you having to know about them to be a part of the group. To try and find where these may exist, it's worth just asking those you work with, your management team or those in your network who already work in the industry you're looking to join.

Consultancy firms regularly offer opportunities to bring companies within an industry together to discuss challenges and opportunities and these forums can be great places to find those in similar roles to yourself in competitor companies. These are often advertised by consultancy companies as something they're doing to bring the industry together on key topics, which benefits them through potential new business and increasing their own awareness of what is important to the companies and industries involved.

These forums, as well as the organisational networks, can be great sources of informal intelligence on benchmarking against companies including on specific approaches to particular issues. The level of openness will vary depending on industry and topic but will often nevertheless provide some useful insights. By attending and being a part of these forums, you may not only be able to increase your own insights from the inputs of others but also be able to add value where your work on the MBA may be exploring topics that are being discussed.

Many MBA courses involve incorporating applied projects to real-world businesses. Some universities proactively engage with businesses to secure opportunities for students on these projects, but you may either need or want to reach out to businesses on your own for these projects. Your industry network is a fundamental part of providing these opportunities and can be a crucial part of helping you to secure employment following the MBA. By being in tune with current industry challenges, you will be able to add more insight to your course, whilst also improving your chances of being able to add value to businesses through applying the content you learn to real-world business problems.

Key takeaway points – internal versus external professional reputation:

Internal reputation

- You can tailor your assignments to your own organisation or a role and organisation you're targeting, which will help to increase the quality of relationships within your network as well as your understanding of the role, organisation and industry. This is crucial in demonstrating the link to your superiors between your MBA and delivering value to your personal development and your company.
- Use opportunities to involve key stakeholders in your assignments, who may have influence over your future career progression and income. Gaining their input will improve your assignments and business acumen whilst also increasing your

visibility and improving your likelihood of securing favourable future opportunities.
- Continue to build your reputation with your previous employer as well as your current employer where it makes sense to do so. Their familiarity with you can be a blessing or a curse but will nevertheless provide opportunities in some circumstances.
- Don't neglect those in your network who may have endorsed company sponsorship for you or have been supportive of your application. They are key advocates to keep on side.
- Make sure you know what the expectations are of you, both whilst you work towards an MBA and following completion – ensure you remain aligned with this expectation to protect your reputation with your stakeholders.
- You have an opportunity to bring as many colleagues along with you as possible. Their support, or lack of it, can make the difference between a successful initiative and a failed one. Make sure you engage with MBA material on how to effectively gain the cooperation of others and seek to involve your colleagues in your work and ideas. Asking for advice and input helps to provide alternative perspectives whilst also gaining an element of buy-in to your progress.
- Remain aware of your wider internal network, which may include family and friends as well as acquaintances from any hobbies you may have, such as societies, sports, or charity work. This may

not only provide opportunities for you, but you may also be able to provide opportunities or advice for others.

External reputation

- The business school may support you, but you need to put in the work to get the most out of external interactions and to build your reputation.
- By reaching out to potential contacts in a business you're interested in, you may be able to form suitable relationships where you can share tailored assignments on the company for input and feedback. Through this, you can increase your visibility whilst also deepening your understanding of the company to support your application.
- In applying for roles in specific companies, if you can, avoid agencies as they will pre-screen applications before submitting yours. By not going through agencies, you remove this pre-screening process as well as not closing yourself off to employers who won't accept applications from agencies.
- You can explore your MBA network even before you start the MBA – LinkedIn is a great place to get to know your future cohort to hit the ground running.
- Your reputation within your cohort whilst on the MBA can help you secure higher marks, through

your interactions with others. By having a good reputation, others may be more willing to engage with you on ideas and perspectives, which in turn will help increase your understanding as well as helping build good working relationships.
- Having a good reputation during the MBA can pay dividends following the course, when you may look to your cohort to explore employment or further networking opportunities.
- With new graduates every year, your network is continually expanding. This presents frequent opportunities to build additional relationships.
- You can use your network to deepen your industry and trend insights to identify potential areas of added value for you and your business. Through this, you can increase your reputation in your own network as an expert in your field.
- Industry networks can be a great way to raise your profile and gain valuable insights. These may be formal or informal groups who you can connect with through existing representatives in your company or through platforms such as LinkedIn.
- Consultancy firms can hold forums for representatives of competitors within industries to discuss key topics. These offer a great way to network with your counterparts in other companies.
- Staying aware of current industry challenges will allow you to add more insight to your course, whilst improving your chances of being able to add value to businesses through applying the

content you learn to real-world business problems.

Chapter Four

Full-time, Part-time, Online?

4.1 Weighing it up – positives and negatives

A full-time course is clearly a significant commitment as well as being, almost by default, higher risk. This is because you may not automatically have a job to go back to, with employee rights and protection in this area varying by country, your company and your own personal agreements. In theory, you should be able to come out of the course more qualified. However, being able to take advantage of this depends on the job market and your ability to sell your new skills and experience through networking and your applications. This can be a tall order as you'll need to be seeking opportunities whilst balancing the demands of the course. As you'll also potentially be returning to the job marketplace after the MBA finishes without a current job to fall back on, you may have limited time to secure a new role before things start to get difficult with living expenses, which could force you into a job you may not have originally wanted.

This is a very real risk for those without a guaranteed job at the end of a full-time course, unless you're in the fortunate position where you can explore other temporary options until you find the role you wanted. Just one of the many potential flexible and temporary examples available to you might be working within a family business. The important part of a potential solution such as this is having access to a reasonable income and an ability for you to demonstrate progression following on from the MBA, so as to continue in enhancing your halo effect for your subsequent job applications.

It goes without saying that not having a job to fall back on can create a really stressful situation and can also set you back if you lose momentum of your career trajectory as a result of taking a less than ideal role out of necessity. Even if you have the time to wait, if you don't have something that reflects well to put on your CV until you find that role you're looking for, this can appear increasingly less favourably to employers as time moves on, who generally don't like to see large gaps in career history. Ultimately, maintaining some sort of job security and a progressive trajectory can be one of the most difficult and stressful aspects of a full-time MBA and does present significant risk for many.

Despite this risk, many people do have a job to come back to at the end of the course which is an undoubtedly great situation to be in. This reduces the potential downside of the full-time option and allows these candidates to make the most of the immersive experience. A drawback to this approach is the lost time of not having professional experience to your name during this time as you'll essentially be taking a career break. You can explain this perception away by some of the practical and soft skill development activities found on full-time MBA courses, such as real-world business projects where you often work with businesses to address strategic problems. With this being said, no matter how you try to sell this, some may still perceive you spending the time essentially in academia and developing fewer professional skills than someone who was in full-time employment. This perception will vary by employer and hiring manager but is still out there. However, the extent to which this view impacts your potential opportunities may depend on your ability to sell the value of your experience on a full-time MBA to those who might not initially see it in the same way as you might like them to.

A full-time MBA with some hands-on project experience in businesses, gained over one to two years may not appear to give as much experience as a part-time or online MBA gained over the same period, whilst gaining almost full or completely full-time professional experience. The ability to put the knowledge into immediate use in a job alongside the MBA, testing out theories and having immediate impact, is much more readily available and can be easier to sell as a higher quality experience once you've completed the MBA. This may not be the case for all industries and roles you're targeting but will be for many, where part-time and online courses are prevalent and valued equally to full-time courses.

Despite these challenges, the full-time course remains an immersive and highly effective experience in developing highly sought-after skills and knowledge in an accelerated timeline. The closeness to fellow students, professors and business leaders and the frequency of interactions with these groups of people often creates a much richer experience than alternative modes of study. This can really help embed learnings on a deeper level through the comparatively higher engagement required of you during the course. Many part-time and online courses replicate elements of this, often through short periods of in-person immersive experiences, but these alternatives struggle to completely replicate the level of prolonged exposure offered by full-time MBA courses.

One of the opportunities that comes with the full-time mode of study is that, due to the immersive experience, you'll more than likely develop a much deeper working relationship with the rest of the cohort. These can be crucial partners who you can begin to rely on for future opportunities, both leading up to and following graduation. Although there may be potentially high risks for you if you're going into a full-time MBA without a job to fall back on, there is strong potential return on investment through the chance of securing a very good job upon graduating. The theory being, as long as you put in the work to make it happen, you're more likely to achieve your goals through the comparatively more immersive experience and stronger network you're likely to have the opportunity to form.

Many full-time MBAs also offer some sort of increased focus on real-world application and practical experience with businesses, who are often affiliated with the business school, whether this is through internships or as part of modules. This real-world application provides great opportunities to network with businesses and explore whether there may be opportunities for you upon graduating. As securing new employment is usually a major focus for those attending the full-time MBA, the business school is likely to also focus on facilitating networking with potential employers and generally be much more geared towards enabling this. Although full-time study can be a higher risk option, it should also be the option most focused and equipped towards getting you to a positive outcome. It's worth thinking through and assessing how apparent this focus and capability is in the business schools you're considering applying to.

Part-time modes of study offered by many institutions can help address the higher-risk situation presented by full-time study. This provides an option which can be the best of both worlds: you'll be getting the face to face immersive experience on a day or two per week whilst still doing your almost full-time role. This allows the opportunity for you to demonstrate the added value of the course more readily to your employer in real-time, by focusing some of your modules or projects on your current workplace. The flip side of this is there will inevitably be more pressure on you to show the value of the MBA, often before you've really got to grips with the material. This can make for quite a high-pressure environment which will be sustained for the majority of the time you're doing both the MBA and working. However, if done well and if you have the time to commit to learning the material whilst also consistently demonstrating and trying to apply it your workplace, the benefits will be clear to your employer and this can really elevate your impact and reputation. This real-world tangible demonstration of benefits will help add weight to your case for progression or pay increases in the future.

A downside of the part-time option is the reliance on your employer's willingness to allow you to cut down your hours in order for you to attend business school. If you do have a willing employer, this can become quite a challenge day to day if there are any high-priority projects which may supersede your studies from your employer's perspective. Most of the time, business schools recognise there is a chance of this conflict occurring and many will offer some flexibility in assessments when needed, but this may not be possible if it extends for any length of time. There's also the chance that although your employer initially agrees to reduced hours, they don't properly put in place the support for the balance of the time you're in business school, leaving you with more work than planned. To try and overcome this, it's worth raising any concern early with your employer before you start and making sure there are checks in place and clear actions that would be taken if the workload becomes too much. How successful this is will depend on the employer and managers involved, but it is worth putting the thought in to reduce potential risks before you go down this route.

Online and distance-learning MBAs are becoming increasingly available but are offered less by the more traditionally super-elite universities. Despite their benefits, negative perceptions of online degrees generally, and online MBAs specifically, can be very commonplace. However, this negative perception is increasingly unfounded due to the progressively advanced offerings from some universities. These emerging elements within online courses should help to overcome previous online programme limitations, which were said to allow limited networking, relationship development and recruitment potential. Although these courses have improved in these areas, you may find you need to drive the outcomes you want from the experience harder than you otherwise might through a full-time course.

These online and distance-learning courses offer flexibility as their main selling point and as a result, can attract a wide range of students with a diverse set of backgrounds. The flexibility can allow you to undertake an MBA completely in your spare time, allowing you to continue to work full-time. This is a massive additional time commitment, with most courses advising around 15 or 20 hours of study per week required to achieve good results, with this varying by person depending on your natural ability. It might also take you longer to get up to speed if you aren't used to writing and the process of completing assignments. Doing the maths on this can show just how much of a commitment it can be – 15 hours might be broken down into 2 hours per weekday and 5 hours at the weekend or 2 hours twice a week followed by 5 or 6 hours on Saturday and Sunday mornings. However you decide to do this, it will need to become your new routine for however many years the course runs for, with consistency in committing to this becoming your key to succeeding.

Some online courses also have the added benefit of offering in-person intensive modules as a hybrid approach within the online distance-learning mode of study. These are a great way to build deeper relationships with the cohort whilst still maintaining flexibility. Quite often, modules that offer this will involve around a week's intensive period of lectures, workshops, networking and skill development activities followed by the assessment some weeks later. One of the reasons students choose full-time courses over online is the face-to-face interaction and real-world relationship building and networking. The fact that some universities are offering this hybrid approach is challenging this perception and opening this mode of study up as a beneficial option for many.

The advantage of having this flexibility can mean that even without an employer supporting you through time or financial commitments, many can still go to business school and secure an MBA. This can be a lifeline for those stuck in careers they aren't enjoying but may otherwise struggle to move away or progress from without developing further skills and experience beforehand. The online or distance-learning mode of study can also be used as a selling point for future job applications, as it demonstrates clear commitment to improving yourself and requires significant prioritisation and time management skills to complete. This was exactly the feedback one of the students in my own cohort received when they successfully secured a new role whilst completing an MBA via the online mode of study. Their commitment and determination was clear to the employer and their willingness to put themselves through the MBA to develop their skills independently of employer support was testament to this and had helped them to stand out from the other applicants.

Balancing your priorities whilst studying via the online mode of study may sound difficult on the face of it and this in itself puts many people off from even trying. However, if you're reasonably consistent in your approach and the amount of time you're putting into the course, you stand every chance of success. The very fact you're putting yourself forward for an MBA can be a real positive for your current and potential employers and can help open doors to new opportunities well before you've even finished the MBA, which you can take full advantage of as you'll still be working full-time. There were countless examples from my own cohort of progression that occurred during the MBA for those within the online mode of study, with many of these strongly linked to the fact those people were on the course and developing themselves.

The flip side to this is with you studying in your spare time over the long-term, any additional workload or pressure can come at significant risk to you maintaining an even balance and keeping up with the workload. In particular, any time-intensive life events may put real strain on you, such as having a baby, moving to a new house, or getting a new job or promotion. As with the part-time mode of study, universities usually appreciate this and will be lenient, but the extent of leniency might not be there for sustained periods. Several people in my cohort did do some of these life-changing events whilst on the course and I did two out of the three myself. I can honestly say I wouldn't change it if I did the whole thing again, but it was pretty intense and my marks did suffer, particularly during a house move. This was purely out of the reduced time for intensive thought I had available to put into studying and interacting with the course content.

Without this interaction with the course content and with others in your cohort, your understanding of the material does begin to wane over time. This is because engaging with the material and your peers is a fundamental part of the learning process which can be hard to replicate through individual study in isolation. Similarly, the skills developed during business school are best formed through a variety of means and by reducing the range of methods you're using to interact with the information, the skills and knowledge won't be formed as easily or reliably. We'll cover the varieties of tools used as learning methods more in Chapter Six, which covers the content and method of delivery from a module on a world-leading MBA course.

Thinking about the part-time and online modes of study in particular, as we mentioned briefly earlier, you may be able to secure new employment leading up to or during your MBA, accelerating your career before you even graduate. This will be easier and much more likely to happen whilst studying for an online MBA, rather than part-time, purely because getting a prospective employer to agree to the same time out of the office needed for part-time study will usually be difficult. However, with online MBAs, a new job is something you're able to pursue independent of your study. Although this has clear benefits, as you're able to realise potential increases in salary sooner, the experience of those on my cohort who managed this was that this added significant amounts of pressure to their work life, their home life and them continuing to deliver to the right standard on the MBA. However, if you're looking to succeed through the MBA process, it's more than likely that you'll be more than happy for some short-term pressure for long-term reward, that will also potentially further increase over time.

All three main modes of study are viable options of gaining a good MBA. At the end of the day, an employer in the future will see that you have an MBA and in the majority of industries likely won't care how you got it. They may not even care which university it came from unless you're making a point about it or trying to use this to enhance the positives of your experience. If at that point, you can demonstrate you have one or two years more professional experience than other applicants as a result of having studied online or part-time, this can be a considerable advantage for you when applying to the vast majority of industries and roles. Part-time or online might not be something you're open to or even might not be an option if you're targeting one of the business schools who don't offer this yet. You may also be specifically looking for the full immersive experience offered by a full-time course which does have its benefits. However, it's worth giving this choice some serious thought and doing the research needed to make sure it will work for you.

When it comes down to the options available, funding is likely to underpin the whole decision process for many. On a basic level, if you're working whilst completing the MBA you won't be losing out on the opportunity of earning an income during that one to two years and are likely to be in a stronger position to negotiate salary at the end of your MBA, from your existing status as being employed. Many people will be self-funding and working full or part-time alongside studies, which offers the chance to come out less debt-burdened than if you were to go all-in and be haemorrhaging money on living costs and fees whilst not earning at all.

For the lucky few, you may have an employer willing to let you study full-time and have a job or even further opportunities waiting for you once you complete the MBA, but generally these opportunities are few and far between. If you do fall into this category, the concern might be more around what other opportunities you might be missing out on by being tied to your employer. In these circumstances, the employer is likely to write some amount of time into your contract following graduation to ensure they see the return on their investment, with fee repayment clauses if you leave before that point. Leaving also presents a risk to your professional reputation after an employer provided such an opportunity, only for you to leave at the first sight of a better deal post-graduation. However, the extent to which this matters to you will depend on the size and culture of the industry and whether you're going to want to maintain a reputation from where you're leaving.

Methods of assessment can vary by institution and mode of study, which will ultimately be very unlikely to be a major decision factor. However, the methods used in different modes of study are worth bearing in mind if you want to play to your strengths or improve on your weaknesses. Assessments can be wide-ranging from short to extended assignments, exams, individual and group presentations, and participation in classes. Specifically, full-time MBA courses will often factor in your participation in classes, with this element often being absent in part-time or online courses. On courses which have several elective modules for you to choose from, you can often see what the method of assessment would be prior to making your choice, allowing you to factor this into your decision if you're concerned about securing the highest marks you can. We'll be exploring ways you can increase your chances of securing high marks in Chapter Seven but for now, it's just worth bearing the methods of assessment in mind when you're comparing courses, depending on your ambitions to either improve your marks or improve your weaknesses.

Key takeaway points – full-time, part-time, online?

Full-time pros

- Provides an immersive and focused experience, allowing you to focus completely on the MBA.

- Allows more exposure to your cohort, professors and business leaders allowing you to more effectively and reliably develop highly sought-after skills and knowledge in an accelerated timeline.
- This comparatively rich experience may allow you more time to focus on building and demonstrating the skills necessary to switch career or industry.
- The ability to develop deeper connections with your external network on the cohort, leading to an increased likelihood of you leaving the course with contacts you can call on to help you seek out employment in your chosen sector.
- If you're able to study full-time and you're aiming to secure a place on one of the traditionally super-elite MBA courses, being willing to pursue this mode of study will bring you one step closer to these courses, which often only offer full-time MBA programmes.
- Many courses will have comparatively more focus on real-world application through affiliated businesses, which can be through modules or internships, allowing you to simultaneously explore opportunities for after your graduation.
- The higher risk nature of full-time study will often result in comparatively more focus by the university on supporting you in securing employment post-MBA. You should investigate the effectiveness and capabilities of business schools in this, but those who do this well can

offer a distinct focused advantage to those studying full-time.

Full-time cons

- May present higher risk if you don't have a job guaranteed on graduation.
- You will be reliant on there being a favourable job market on graduating.
- Post-graduation, the longer it takes to secure a job in your sought-after field, the more pressure you may be under to accept something that is less than what you hoped, which can be damaging for your career trajectory.
- The time you spend on the course will be time you aren't gaining professional experience directly in the workplace, which may be favoured less by some employers, when compared to somebody who gained more experience whilst studying part-time or online.

Part-time pros

- The opportunity to continue gaining professional experience in the workplace whilst gaining an MBA.
- If you are self-funding, you will usually be able to graduate with significantly less debt than the full-time mode of study.
- There is no need to wait until you complete the MBA to change jobs.

- You may be in a stronger position to negotiate salary on post-MBA roles, as you will already be in employment.
- There will be less pressure to find a new role post-graduation within a certain time period, as you will already be earning an income in your current role.
- The ability to apply the theories from your MBA directly to your everyday work, demonstrating your increasing value to your employer in real-time.

Part-time cons

- It may be more difficult to get support from your employer to take this route.
- If workload increases in your job, you may lose time you would have spent attending your MBA course if your employer deems this as less important than company work or if there are high priority deliverables.
- The support your employer provides may contractually tie you into working for them for many more years post-graduation, with fee repayment clauses if you were to leave before this.
- Employer expectations may be higher, with beliefs that you will quickly begin to apply MBA theory to practice and deliver results quickly, adding to the pressure you will be under. Any deviation from expectations as a result of this may begin to harm your reputation.

Online pros

- The most flexible way to achieve an MBA, allowing you to fit studies around other professional or personal commitments.
- Allows you to pursue an MBA whilst working full-time, maximising your professional workplace experience and income during your studies.
- If you are self-funding, you will usually be able to graduate with significantly less debt than the full-time mode of study and even less debt than the part-time mode of study.
- Minimal employer support is required as you will be doing it purely in your own time and can do it without funding if you are able to support this yourself.
- Can be used to demonstrate a commitment to developing yourself as well as excellent time management and prioritisation skills to potential employers.
- As with the part-time option, you will have the ability to start new employment prior to or during the MBA if you find suitable opportunities.

Online cons

- Face-to-face contact may be reduced compared to other modes of study, which can impact on how deep of a connection you can make with those on the cohort.
- Requires a high amount of self-discipline to consistently commit to spending the time

required on the course (15 or 20 hours of study per week required to achieve good results, with this varying by person depending on your natural ability).
- May only be offered by limited universities and few of the traditionally super-elite MBA courses.
- May be perceived less favourably by some hiring managers, resulting in a potential need to overcome negative perceptions in some situations.

Chapter Five

Prioritisation and Planning

5.1 Priorities

Research by the Graduate Management Admissions Council showed cost and debt needed to fund an MBA as being the largest drivers behind stopping people from applying, closely followed by uncertain job prospects[5]. However, the extent to which this applies to you will likely depend on whether you're targeting the top US business schools or more elite international schools with high tuition fees. I say this because there are such a wide variety of MBA courses out there that for the majority of people wanting to meet their professional goals, it is perfectly possible to find an MBA course which fits with your aspirations and doesn't involve spending huge sums of money. Don't get me wrong, there are still likely to be significant sums involved but if you're willing to prioritise an MBA as something you want to achieve, and think

---

[5] https://www.gmac.com/-/media/files/gmac/research/admissions-and-application-trends/demand-for-mba-and-business-masters-programsinsights-on-candidate-decision-making-summary-reportmbac.pdf

carefully about the cost in relation to the value it will provide for you in achieving your goals, it can be done.

It may also be the case that although cost and debt prevent some people from applying in that particular application round, they either then go on to commit to saving towards this goal or secure opportunities for other funding and eventually cost and debt don't become prohibitive. There are so many options available to achieving an MBA that the majority of people who are committed can work towards this goal and eventually achieve it. It may take some people longer than others, but it is still a realistic ambition for most.

As for the potential uncertainty in job prospects, this is harder to address as it is highly dependent on your personal circumstances and the industry and roles you're targeting. This book should help in framing some of the considerations you should be evaluating in trying to establish whether an MBA equals better job prospects for your situation, but the more research you can do on this specific to your position, the better. Generally an MBA will often help, or viewed another way certainly won't be a hindrance to you, but in order to work out how much of a risk it might be for you, you need to put in the time to carry out extensive research.

My own journey to achieving an MBA started 10 years before I ended up graduating, when I decided to pursue one as I'd established that it would likely help my career in my chosen field and the risk was one worth taking. At this point, I was in debt and renting a room in a house-share and it felt like I'd set the bar almost too high for myself. Prior to this, I'd failed my first attempt at an undergraduate degree but found my way during my second attempt. However, the journey wasn't easy – I'd come out of school with average grades and my unpractised writing abilities were picked up on in university. However, I worked on my academic writing ability and slowly but surely improved.

Once I had done the research which confirmed an MBA would be the eventual best path forward, for the greatest chance of success I knew I'd need to improve on every prerequisite before I got to the point of being able to apply. Through taking a regular balanced view on my strengths and weaknesses and taking feedback onboard, I targeted improving on these through SMART (specific, measurable, attainable, realistic, time-bound) goals. After a few years of focused improvement, I was able to demonstrate adequate professional competence to the level required in respected business schools. All the while during this time, I was consistently saving for the tuition fees – a slow process given that I was also trying to pay off debt and save for a deposit on a house. In the end, I ended up paying for the tuition through a mixture of student loans and savings and I'd encourage anyone thinking about doing an MBA to look at all possible funding options and what impacts these might have on your post-graduation finances before committing.

This isn't to say that completing the MBA was my only goal, but it was a big piece of the puzzle for my own career, particularly in giving me the best possible chance at lasting success and an accelerated, upward career trajectory. The reason I wanted to share this aspect of my own story was that ultimately, whether you choose an MBA as a route to your career progression or not, you can always improve your situation with hard work, commitment and consistency. If I hadn't have chosen to do an MBA, I'm sure my own opportunities would have naturally steadily improved anyway as a result of practising these traits. However, I do credit career progression to the MBA, as for me, this led to my knowledge and capabilities increasing at a rapid rate, which subsequently led to greater opportunities being presented much earlier than they would otherwise have been.

Your general priorities in life need to be weighed up against your desire for career progression and how an MBA could fit into this. The next section on time, family life and relationships, as well as the following section after this on opportunity cost, will go deeper into these elements. In terms of priorities, it's worth taking a long-term view on how an MBA might help you. Business schools tend to focus heavily on salary increases only a few years out from graduation and a few notable alumni. It's worth thinking about where you want to be five or even ten years or more from graduating and how this ambition fits into your life plans. Clearly you can't plan everything, especially to any degree of accuracy that far into the future. However, having a rough long-term view will help you try to determine your potential return on investment from doing an MBA, which we'll cover in more detail in the opportunity cost section.

Key takeaway points – prioritisation and planning

- For the majority of people wanting to achieve their personal and professional aspirations, it is perfectly possible to find an MBA course which both aligns with your goals and also doesn't involve spending huge sums of money.
- Your potential job prospects and the benefit you might hope to gain from an MBA need careful consideration – you need to put in the time to researching how much of a risk seeking an MBA may pose to you and if these risks are worth taking in the context of potential benefits.
- Whether you choose an MBA as a route to furthering your career progression or not, you can always improve your personal and professional situation with hard work, commitment and consistency.
- Take a long-term view on potential MBA benefits. You may not be able to accurately predict your journey for as far out as the next ten years, but this vision based on your research of what is possible and what would be valuable for you will help in determining your potential return on investment.

5.2 Time, family life and relationships

This is one aspect very few people spoke about before the MBA but the impact of doing an MBA on your family life and relationships quickly becomes apparent after you start – it can very much be a joint commitment. If you're working on your MBA full-time, this intensive experience will require networking in the evenings and work during evenings and weekends, with some tight deadlines. There will undoubtedly be times when family life and relationships get put on hold which can put tremendous pressure on even the strongest of relationships.

Similarly, on the part-time or online distance-learning modes of study, if you're spending an additional 15 hours per week on your MBA that you weren't previously, that time needs to come from somewhere. It can't usually come from work, so it comes from the time you were previously spending with friends, family and partners. Even if you're doing the part-time mode of study, where your employer may be allowing you time to attend the course, you'll likely still need to commit significant time outside of this to work on assignments or group tasks.

Routine and boundaries can be a great help in these circumstances for some, particularly where you might need to balance childcare or other commitments. This might be dedicating mornings at the weekend to MBA work and having the afternoons and evenings off to spend maintaining relationships, or certain nights of the week where you commit to not doing assignments. Either way, this time can be essential downtime, not just for you but for those in your life. This boundary setting can also be really beneficial in focusing your effort and getting the most from your time. As Parkinson's law goes: work expands so as to fill the time available for its completion.

Doing an MBA can be a life-changing decision and will require the appropriate time investment it needs to successfully complete. It's worth factoring in the MBA commitment in the context of your wider life circumstances. For example, for many on my own cohort it was a blessing to have started the MBA before having children, which may have reduced the time available to spend with them. Similarly, many of those on the full-time MBA had few ties and were more likely to be fully mobile, which helped to maximise opportunities during and following the MBA, from both the amount of time available to commit to exploring opportunities and flexibility in potential employment locations. Although some students such as these had comparatively fewer commitments, more often than not, you will find that students do have families, challenging jobs and other responsibilities that they balance with their MBA. This is definitely possible and was the case for a large number of students in my business school who chose the flexible modes of study to minimise the impact the MBA would have on childcare. You will find that because of the typical demographics of the cohort, most students will have families of their own and they are no less able to use an MBA to help in achieving their personal and professional goals.

Key takeaway points- time, family life and planning

- Doing an MBA can be a joint commitment with friends, family and partners, with these relationships often having less time invested in them out of necessity.
- Routine and boundaries with some essential downtime can help focus your time spent on the MBA whilst helping maintain relationships.
- Consider your wider life circumstances and what it would mean on a personal level to spend the time on an MBA that you could spend elsewhere in your life. It is worth thinking about this in the context of available modes of study and if one of these may more closely align with your personal commitments outside of the MBA.

5.3 Opportunity cost and funding

Opportunity cost occurs when an option is chosen from alternative opportunities. The cost is incurred by not enjoying the benefits of the choices not made. In the last section, we've mentioned one of the softer, more qualitative, opportunity costs from a family and relationships perspective. In considering this, we've factored in the age and circumstances which might influence the way you fit an MBA into your life, including the mode of study you choose and how you might balance your priorities. A further opportunity cost lies in financial terms which also needs careful consideration. We'll firstly look at this in more quantitative terms but it will ultimately also tie into your longer-term work-life balance ambitions, if these play a part in your overall goals, as this will likely impact your return on the initial investment of the MBA itself. Weighing this up may also help you set a limit as to what might make sense as an amount to spend on pursuing your MBA.

Most people pursue an MBA to help secure a promotion or move industries, whether that's achieved through increased business knowledge and credibility, networking, or a combination of these. As a result, there is usually some sort of clear opportunity cost at play, whether from a financial perspective, a personal perspective or mixture of both. From a purely cost and career development perspective, these can be broken down into several key areas:

- The cost of the course itself and the alternative uses you might have for those funds. Traditional other uses of large amounts of money for long-term return on investment might be investing in the stock market or buying property to let. If you're taking on debt to fund your studies, the option becomes whether or not to take on the debt and the impact of this on any other goals or opportunities you may have available.
- The cost of taking time out of professional employment if you're undertaking a full-time MBA.
- Your specific career focus – this may be the opportunity cost of pursuing another industry or

not pursuing it and the time in which this occurs relative to you pursuing an MBA. For example, you might be pursuing a comparatively more lucrative industry than your current one. In this situation, the sooner you make the transition, in theory, the higher potential return you might see through your ability to earn more from an earlier point in time. However, this one is more difficult to quantify as it relies on you making a number of assumptions on a future career which will inevitably depend on a wide range of variables.

There is a further opportunity cost which also acts a risk, which is the risk relating to workload on part-time and online MBA courses. If this workload impacts on the time you can spend on your day to day job, there is an opportunity cost to the additional time you would have spent on your standard everyday work. The risk lies in whether there are any negative consequences of this or any opportunities you might have missed if you were able to put an additional few hours per week into your day job, rather than having to prioritise your MBA work.

I know for some people who have completed online MBAs, this has been particularly difficult and they have had to sacrifice the quality of their MBA work as a result of investing less time than was ideal due to work commitments. This was a more favourable option as opposed to risking minor reputation damage in their current work as a result of clocking off at 5pm and transitioning to work on their MBA straight away, irrelevant of current workplace challenges. For these people, quite often this conflicting requirement was relatively short-lived, lasting a few weeks, and they could often re-prioritise and catch up on their MBA once the higher than normal work obligations had reduced. Although getting this balance right was challenging for these students, the ability to work flexibly is a key benefit of the online MBA which does allow for week-to-week variability in effort and time invested.

The opportunity cost of focusing on the MBA, rather than your work, for an additional few hours per week might be the difference between a promotion and no promotion over the course of a year or two. Again, this is difficult to quantify but worth bearing in mind. The extent to which this risk will apply to you will highly depend on how engaged and supportive your employer is and their ability to see the benefit of you spending the time on the MBA as opposed to directly business related activity. Your ability to influence your employer and successfully demonstrate that your effort on the MBA is a long-term investment for them will help to minimise the risk of your employer seeing your invested time on the MBA as a short-term negative for the business.

The MBA marketing material that universities often use claim high post-MBA salaries and career progression, but very few directly prove correlation of that success to the MBA. This is because it often becomes difficult to pin down exactly how gaining an MBA helped someone to progress in their career and may come down to perception or a loose causation at best. Although it will likely be the case there was a good link in many instances, correlation does not equal causation in all cases and it will be hard to identify exactly what aspect of the MBA provided the most benefit. There are plenty of people who would likely have seen some sort of progression without an MBA, through consistency, hard work and a commitment to improving themselves and their work. As these are traits generally found within anyone thinking about doing an MBA (which includes you by the very fact you're reading this book), you stand a fair chance of achieving SMART goals that you put your mind to, with or without an MBA. Despite this, MBAs more often than not continue to present a very effective way of achieving accelerated personal and professional development, but working out where the best value for money will be for your particular situation is your next step.

Starting with the cost of the course itself, you need to weigh this up as holistically as you can. If you're looking at full-time courses, include fees, text books, lack of earnings during the period of the course (and for a time afterwards whilst you're potentially still job-seeking), as well as estimated cost of social events and networking during the course. It's also worth bearing in mind any travel or accommodation you might need for any specific modules which might be held abroad. Try to go more towards highest case on these costs as you don't want to underestimate them in your analysis. If it turns out you over-estimated, it will be in your favour, rather than you struggling to find extra funds at a later date.

For part-time and online courses, you will definitely need most of the above elements but can exclude lost earnings. We can also remove cost of living and general accommodation from this on the assumption you'd be paying this anyway and it wouldn't be an additional specific cost. However, if there is a significant difference between what this would be normally and anything which you'd have to pay additionally to attend the course, it's worth including this in your analysis. You also need to factor in any interest on any loans you're planning to take out to fund your course as this can be substantial. Also consider if the repayments on these loans post-graduation are likely to pose any risk for you or lost opportunities that you're unwilling to sacrifice, such as not going on holiday for a few years whilst you're paying them off or potentially postponing a house purchase. Again, this assumes a worst-case scenario that you might not secure any sort of salary increase straight away but this is a safer assumption for the purposes of your planning. If you do secure salary increases soon after your MBA, these will be a bonus. Taking this approach should reduce the pressure you will be under and allow you to take a longer-term view in any career decisions, rather than just chasing a higher paying role.

Once you've worked out what this total number is for the cost of attending the courses you're looking at, you now need to consider the potential opportunities available to you if you weren't to go to business school. Could this money be put to use buying property to rent out or investing in the stock market and what would this likely give you as an alternative use of these funds? This can be based on both financial aspects and more qualitative aspects, such as quality of life or personal goals. How does the risk of your alternative options for the money compare to the risk of you not seeing a return on your potential new skills, which you would have for the rest of your life? Will using this money towards an MBA mean that you need to delay a home purchase or other significant life event? How do these risks compare and how sure are you that having an MBA will deliver the results you're looking for? It's key to think about this potential gain on a long-term horizon. Although there may be an initial spike of benefit immediately following an MBA, the skills and, if maintained, your network will be present for the rest of your career.

In doing your assessment, the research into your potential business schools combined with the industries and jobs you're targeting is crucial. If the consensus of alumni or people you've spoken to in the roles or industry you're pursuing is that you'll likely need an MBA, or it would at least be very beneficial, then this would add weight onto this being the right way to go. However, if the feedback is mixed or unclear, the risk of your opportunity cost being greater becomes higher. In this instance, you will need to make a more risk-adjusted decision, depending on your appetite for risk and whether your circumstances realistically allow for it, without threatening your standard of living beyond what you might be willing to accept. If the risk of an MBA not actually returning much value for your situation is high, you may want to consider a less prestigious and less costly

MBA programme which might offer some of the benefits you were looking for without the full high-risk investment.

Alternatively, you may decide pursuing an MBA isn't for you at all and you're better off saving the money for something else and pursuing the development opportunities you were looking for through other means, such as self-taught learning, networking events or work-based development plans. Although you won't get the halo effect benefits from this approach, or the network and intensity of experience, which help support the accelerated capability developments people derive from MBAs, you will still be able to replicate some elements of the knowledge over time. This will require the same consistency and dedication, as well as a passion to learn.

Whilst you can teach yourself much of what is taught in MBA courses, it's how you will learn that will be different and it is this way of learning that can form a large part of how the skills are developed and your resulting competency. As we covered right at the beginning of the book in the introduction, the evidence suggests that MBAs and advanced degrees in general are becoming more commonplace. If you're ambitious in your professional goals, you will likely find that you will need to continue to develop your skills throughout your career whether you commit to an MBA or not. As a result, depending on your aspirations, there may be an additional argument for you pursuing an MBA as a way to make sure you stay ahead of the curve and have a higher chance of securing tangible benefits earlier in your career.

If you did decide to explore other options, one of the best ways to discover similar material in a comparable way to the MBA experience would be to find like-minded people and engage on the topics, whether that's through networking groups or work-based groups. One of the key skills you develop during an MBA is how to engage with a lot of material, on a complex topic, in a short space of time and be able to take on board a range of conflicting views and ideas to navigate to an effective solution. Once you arrive at this effective solution, another key skill is in efficiently articulating this to a team and bringing them on-side with your idea using a compelling argument and logical reasoning. So, if there are any other ways of developing these skills in this way, they would certainly help to replicate some of the MBA learning environment and skill development. However, to do this effectively, it will still take time and effort and there will be an opportunity cost, but you would not have the benefits of having an official MBA to your name.

In terms of judging the potential benefit of your identified target MBA courses as opposed to the returns from other uses of the money, you can start in gauging this by looking at both the pre-MBA salary of the courses you're applying to in comparison to the post-MBA salaries. Consider what industries the cohort was made up of if you have access to the information and what the salaries are generally like in those professions. It's worth exploring this on a deeper level for your own current and target profession and role. You can explore this further by using LinkedIn which allows you to filter on the MBA graduates of specific universities. Making use of this feature, you can search to find people who may have previously been in your current role and find out where they moved to and the timescales involved. A quick Google search will give you some guides on their salaries in subsequent roles. Clearly, there is a lot more to an individual's progression than just the MBA in isolation and salaries can definitely vary by company and individual, but it does give you a rough guide of realistic career trajectories for your specific situation.

In doing this assessment, be sure to get a good sample size of people who may give a guide to rough career trajectories. Remember the salary myth: the advertised average post-graduation salary will somehow happen automatically, just because you now hold an MBA? Well, there were a few people who graduated from my cohort who were perfectly happy in their current role and pursued an MBA purely for self-development reasons. For these people, climbing the corporate ladder and making as much money as possible wasn't a priority and that's obviously absolutely fine – just not very helpful if that's your priority and you're using them as examples! Similarly, there were others who weren't willing to compromise on certain aspects of their lifestyle to maximise their opportunities (such as location) and this impacted on their potential career path as they lived in remote areas with fewer available options to progress into senior level jobs.

Assuming you decided the opportunity cost would be worth it to pursue an MBA in your situation, your next step is to return to the advantages and disadvantages presented by the different modes of study available to you in the courses you're considering. Throughout this book we have talked about the situations where you may want to pursue a full-time MBA and despite the many benefits, there is no denying that there is a significant opportunity cost presented in studying full-time. This was highlighted to me through an example of two people who achieved an MBA at my own university, through two different modes of study at the same time as myself. Although this example is a specific one from my cohort from two people who I know well, it perfectly captures the very real challenges between modes of study which can be experienced in any business school that offers different ways of gaining an MBA.

     Both students graduated at the same time via different modes of study. We'll call these two people Student A and Student B. Student A had begun working towards their MBA a year prior to Student B via an online distance-learning route. They transitioned industries not long after starting the MBA and in doing so moved into a more senior position. Throughout the course, they were able to apply concepts in real-time, slowly but surely building reputation and knowledge within their business, which they were new to, having joined at the beginning of the MBA. On speaking to this person about their experiences around the industry switch, the fact they had started the MBA was a strong potential contributing factor to them securing the role. The feedback from the employer following their interview had been that it showed their commitment to improving their skills. Although Student A didn't know just how much this contributed to their successful employment, they did think it helped their halo effect. In terms of return on investment, by the end of the course, from the research I did on the typical salaries between their role before and after moving industries at the start of the MBA, the salary increase would more than pay for the cost of the MBA over the two year course.

On the other hand, Student B studied via the full-time mode of study. They had similar pre-MBA experience to Student A in level of seniority and number of years in employment since their undergraduate degree. Student B paid more for the privilege of studying full-time, due to the comparatively higher MBA fees, and wasn't earning for the 12 months whilst on the course. Post-MBA, they had a stressful time looking for jobs which took several months despite significant and consistent networking both during and following the MBA. They then secured a role at the same level of seniority as Student A, but two years later than Student A had secured it.

Did Student B attribute a full-time MBA to securing the position? They definitely thought it played a part. Could they have done it without an MBA? Possibly not. However, comparing situations between Student A and B, both hold the same MBA on paper and are initially at the same career level post-MBA. Student A has been at that level for two years gaining experience whilst Student B hasn't. If both students were in the same department of the same company, which one is more likely to have the most experience on paper and in reality? Student B may be able to bring some experience from the MBA into their work, but it takes time to learn the ins and outs of a role and company properly. Although their comparative experience might balance out over the long-term, Student B wouldn't have the comparable hands-on experience that Student A would have initially gained.

This leads us into the time element of opportunity cost relating to career advancement earlier in a career. If you can progress into a senior role at an early stage, you will not only be paid a larger salary sooner but will also begin gaining comparatively more senior experience earlier on. This is a fundamental way people progress into very senior positions over the long-term. Relating this to the example we looked at above, we can see it shows Student A to be in a much more favourable position for potential long-term advancement.

Thinking about this in the context of mode of study and when you do your MBA can be important to your career trajectory, as by doing the MBA earlier, you will often have the opportunity to progress into more senior roles sooner. This has the benefit of strengthening your career trajectory early in your career, giving you a strong base to further build on. Despite the benefits of this early timing of an MBA, taking a different approach can also bring significant benefits. Timing an MBA in the middle of a career can also form an invaluable part of restarting and boosting well-established careers which may be experiencing a lull or have stagnated.

Many people can be concerned about macroeconomic factors including the state of the future job market when they're weighing up the costs and potential risk in doing an MBA. Having an MBA can actually offset some of this risk. If the job market was to become more challenging, which it may well do, having an MBA will put you at the top of the pile in terms of potential applicants and help you meet the requirements if it's a prerequisite. Thinking about your value as a prospective employee and how this might differ between having an MBA and not having one is likely to give some indication on whether it might be worth pursuing in light of your personal circumstances. Similarly, if you're looking to progress, how easy is this likely to be with and without an MBA in your chosen field? In all likelihood, for most career paths and average MBA costs, the benefit of an MBA over your lifetime will far outweigh the cost. However, weighing this up is a crucial part of ensuring you're making the right decision for you.

Key takeaway points – opportunity cost and funding:

- Opportunity cost occurs when an option is chosen from alternative opportunities. The cost is incurred by not enjoying the benefits of the choices not made.
- Think about the prospects and impacts presented between different modes of study. Considerations relating to this might include the following:
    - When you start your MBA journey.

- Whether you take time out of employment.
- Whether you may see risk in your current employment through time invested.
- When you may look to transition industries.
- The cost differences between the different courses themselves.
- Consider how the opportunity cost of the course relates to the following:
    - Alternative uses of the funds that would be required.
    - The time required in your own situation.
    - Whether there may be other ways you can gain the experience you need in order to achieve your goals.
- The timing of your MBA journey can significantly impact your career trajectory and ability to maximise your opportunities. Being aware of this can allow you to tailor your approach and prioritise your goals.
- Assess the potential return on investment an MBA might provide for you by researching your targeted career paths and those already in the positions you want to pursue.

Chapter Six

Content Overview from a World-Leading MBA

6.1 Content overview

Now we'll take a look at the leadership and management module from a world-leading MBA to give you a guide on how you might spend your time and what the content looks like. We'll explore this module in particular as although it may be named differently from university to university, the subjects covered form a core part of what an MBA teaches. Although the individual concepts and methods taught will vary between MBA courses and potentially over time, it is a good example to provide an overview of the method of learning on this universal subject of challenge and opportunity. As we're working through this, it's worth trying to judge the value you might be able to gain from a similar experience.

Firstly, we'll start with a rough guide on the amount of time required and how this is spent. This will vary from person to person and between universities, as well as the mode of study. You also may not want or need to invest this amount of time in your experience (for a variety of reasons) and we will cover this in more detail in the effort versus goals section of Chapter Seven. However, the time-split below was a minimum for my own personal experience and was applicable if you were starting out with an average base level understanding of the concepts and wanting to get the most from a typical module, as well as securing reasonably high marks by the standards of a very well-respected institution. This is based on the principle that you get out what you put in to the experience and on the assumption you can successfully get to grips with the material and demonstrate your ability to engage with the information in a critical and holistic way. Although this detail is based on my own experience, I also found from speaking with others that over time from year to year, the methods used and topics covered in an MBA don't actually change that much overall. So, although this is an example, it will likely be reasonably representative of a standard core MBA module.

- 50 hours of reading (journal articles, book extracts, case studies, news articles, industry papers) and watching videos (such as TED talks and YouTube videos).
    - Purpose: understand concepts and support discussion.
- 100 hours of total interactive learning (lectures, industry talks and visits, seminars, workshops, interviews, personal and group practical activities, presentations and dedicated self-reflection).

- Purpose: embed learnings through engagement with the material and the cohort.
- Networking naturally occurs throughout these activities with opportunities for you to seek out individuals who you may want to engage with throughout your course.
- 50-100 hours of assessment preparation and creation.
  - Purpose: demonstrate criticality and competence in the material covered.

The total time spent on this whole module was approximately 200-250 hours. This is likely to represent somewhere around 10% of the total MBA mark and work required.

Moving on from how you might spend your time, we will delve a little deeper into the content. To make this as insightful as possible, this is broken down into high-level subject areas with examples of where these topics might involve some form of interactive learning or engagement. These active elements are highlighted in bold. The methods used when interacting with the material are the heart of where value comes from when doing an MBA as these approaches help to properly embed the concepts and skills into your standard ways of working. The opportunities provided for networking and engagement with others on and around the module concepts act to further embed the learnings and develop your relationships with the cohort.

Perspectives of leadership

- **Industry guest interviews** on what it takes to lead in a VUCA (volatile, uncertain, complex and ambiguous) world.
- **Attend workshop** on perceptions of leadership and how it can be defined. **Discuss** famous leaders, their approaches and cohort perceptions of their effectiveness. **Reflect** and **discuss** with others on the course.
- **Lecture** outlining a leadership model, identifying how to improve organisational effectiveness through leadership. **Group activity** applying this model to a personally known organisation. Findings shared with the cohort through **informal presentation** for discussion and input.
- **Reflect** on your personal leadership experiences to form a baseline to revisit later in the course. Identification of leadership experiences which have shaped your perceptions and strengths in personal leadership capability. Outline areas to explore further personal growth opportunities.
- **Read journals** on transactional, transformational and servant styles of leadership. **Informal presentation** sharing your personal understanding and experiences with the cohort of organisations you have worked in where these forms of leadership were found, how they were demonstrated and the strengths and weaknesses of these approaches for the situations in which they were used.

- **Group practical activity** analysing a case study on task and relationship orientation in leadership.
- **Reflect** on task and relationship orientation in those close to you or famous examples, analysing the effectiveness of approaches for their situations and ways they could improve.
- **Personal activity to interview** a select few contacts on their perceptions of leadership, discussing whether this differs from academic theory. **Reflect** on whether these perceptions were consistent and how close they were to your own personal views on leadership.
- **Group discussion** on the findings from interviews and perceptions of leadership in the context of the material covered so far and personal experiences. **Presentation** of these findings back to the group.
- **Read case study** on a leadership example in a challenging situation, identifying ways the person could have improved on their approach.
- **Reflect** on how you can incorporate some of the theories and perceptions of leadership into your own leadership approach.

Power, influence and conflict

- **Analyse** perspectives on political leadership and the use and misuse of power to gain the commitment of others, including ethical considerations. **Present** these findings back to the group for **discussion.**

- **Read journals** on the sources of power (power bases). **Group discussion** on where examples of these sources of power being used can be seen from current events in the news and popular culture.
- **Reflect** on personal experiences of the sources of power, as well as in the context of business relationships you have had in the past or currently have now.
- **Analyse** case studies involving ethical and unethical leadership. **Reflect** on the ethics of your own leadership. **Group discussion** on what made these approaches ethical and unethical.
- **Industry guest speakers** on ethical leadership and what this means to them and their organisations.
- **Read journals and industry papers** on the use of stakeholder mapping to assess power and interest. **Personal activity** to create a power/interest stakeholder map during an organisational change, identifying how and where relationship management could have been improved.
- **Read journals and industry papers** on intrinsic and extrinsic motivation and Maslow's hierarchy of needs. **Personal activity** to apply these theories to an organisational and personal situation you have previously experienced.
- **Read case studies** on examples of employee motivation.

- **Reflect** on how you might improve your own use of power and influence to build your leadership capabilities.

Leadership and management in organisational change

- **Read journals, case studies and industry papers** on examples of when organisational change has failed to produce the desired results.
- **Group discussion** on how to successfully manage change using examples from your previous personal experiences to demonstrate how challenges were overcome.
- **Seminar** and **discussion** on examples of effective leadership during organisational change initiatives and how these cases relate to the material covered so far.
- **Read journals and industry papers** on how to effectively lead change, including the need for adaptability in strategy formation and implementation.
- **Industry guest speakers** on leadership during change management and practical examples of how leaders have effectively implemented change in their organisations.
- **Read journals** on ethical leadership considerations within organisational change.
- **Attend workshop** on a scenario of a challenging organisational change situation. **Discuss** ways to

approach the problem based on the material covered so far and your personal experiences.

Leadership development

- **Read journals** on models that can be used for leadership development and **reflect** on where you fit personally within these models, considering the perceptions others may have of you.
- **Industry guest speakers** on the capabilities leaders of the future will need.
- **Personal activity** to seek feedback from colleagues or friends on your own leadership strengths and opportunities for further development.
- **Case studies** of leadership examples where leaders have developed through a crisis situation.
- **Group practical activity** on ways to assess leadership, including ways companies assess leadership through application processes.
- **Read journals and industry papers** on personal and organisational leadership branding. **Reflect** on how this applies to your own brand and the branding of organisations you have worked for and with.
- **Group discussion** on personal reflections and learnings.

Organisational and personal communication

- **Read journals** on the relationship between communication and leadership, focusing on how gender and cultural diversity, as well as differences in communication styles, can create challenges in practising influencing behaviours and create potential conflict.
- **Group discussion** on what attributes make a good communicator, with examples from popular culture, famous leaders and your personal experiences.
- **Read case studies and historic news articles** on famous corporate and individual communication failures which resulted in significant financial and reputational impact.
- **Read journal articles** on formal and informal organisational communication.
- **Read industry papers and journal articles** on communication as a manager.
- **Group discussion** on personal reflections and learnings on how the concepts covered so far apply to communication in the workplace.
- **Personal activity** on applying communication concepts to messages, inferring meaning from the verbal and non-verbal communication of others.
- **Group activity and discussion,** exploring the interpersonal, organisational and cultural barriers to effective communication in a **case study**, including how they may be overcome.

- **Watch videos** on non-verbal communication and body language, including power poses, and **reflect** on your own experiences of non-verbal communication and how it can influence the perceptions of others, including across cultural boundaries.
- **Read industry papers, journals and watch videos** on rhetoric, the rhetorical appeals of logos, pathos and ethos and their use in leadership examples.
- **Reflect** on good and poor uses of rhetoric in your experiences within organisations and how rhetoric can be used for more effective management and leadership communication.

Organisational culture

- **Read journals** on culture, including Schein's three levels of organisational culture.
- **Watch videos and group discussion** on cultural norms and practices, the challenges these can provide for international business relationships and how HR professionals can support.
- **Watch videos and read industry papers** on Hofstede's five categories of national culture.
- **Read case studies** on communication issues and organisational challenges resulting from cultural differences. **Reflect** on how training could be designed to overcome similar situations and how Hofstede's five categories of national culture can be applied to understand cultural differences.

- **Read journals** critiquing Hofstede's five categories and **reflect** on whether these criticisms are fair.
- **Read journals** on culture within organisations and how this can be encouraged or discouraged through processes and structure. **Group discussion** on personal experiences of culture development within organisations.
- **Read journals** on the relationship between organisational culture and performance.
- **Personal practical activity and group discussion** on improving culture within a challenging **case study** situation.
- **Reflect** on your own management style in the context of individual and organisational cultural considerations and how you might improve on your approach.

Human resource management

- **Read journal and book extract** on the differences between human resource management and personnel management, the nature of employment relationships and the current challenges facing businesses in this area.
- **Watch video** identifying external influences on the employment relationship and the expectations which can be formed outside of contractual obligations (the psychological contract).

- **Read industry paper** on high and low commitment employment relationships and **reflect** on where organisations you have experienced fit on this scale. **Reflect** on what the impact was of this level of commitment for you and others in the business.
- **Read case studies** of disciplinary scenarios and **share** your views with the cohort for **discussion** on what was handled well and what could be improved on.
- **Group practical activity** outlining an approach to a challenging human resource management situation.
- **Share** an example with the cohort of a difficult human resource example you have had to overcome in your previous experience and how you managed this. In the context of any new learnings you have gained, **reflect** on how you might change your approach.
- **Read journals** on how human resource management is influenced through recruitment practices and how strategies for effectively managing capabilities can be adopted, including through candidate sourcing, screening and selection.
- **Read case study** on situations where employment can influence the labour market and **reflect** on ways this could be approached or overcome.
- **Read journals and case studies** on performance reviews and **share** your views to questions on best practice with the cohort for **discussion**.

- **Read journals, watch video and read case study** on the relationship between motivation and reward and recognition, including performance related pay and the potential for bias within this process. **Reflect** on how the case study example could have been approached to help ensure the continued motivation of an employee in a difficult situation.
- **Read journals, industry papers and case studies** on managing equality and diversity through human resource management and overcoming discrimination in the workplace. **Personal practical activity** to improve the approach to a challenging situation for a company trying to overcome discrimination in the workplace through re-training.
- **Read case study** on bullying and harassment in the workplace and **reflect** on questions regarding the situation and approach taken.
- **Reflect** on effective management and leadership in your own previous organisations, including the below:
    - How you might have improved on the approaches used both generally and in specific circumstances.
    - How you might work differently in the future to develop high-performing teams and foster a high-commitment culture.
    - How organisational culture impacted on your success.

- How recognition and reward methods could have been used or could be used in the future to secure the cooperation of others.

Assessment

In this particular example of a module from my own MBA experience, the below is how your understanding, application of the material covered and critical thinking would be assessed.

1. Assessed self-reflection on key personal learnings from the module and how they will help your personal management and leadership approaches (25% of the overall module mark).
2. Approach and improvement plan for a case study of a challenging organisational situation (75% of the overall module mark).

This overview should have given you a good idea on the areas of focus for this module within a highly regarded MBA course and how undergoing something similar might benefit your capability development. However, it should go without saying that although this is an overview, actually going through the motions of these activities in person will give you a completely different experience of the topic than just reading a summary! This goes all the way back to our myth that there are other ways to replicate the MBA knowledge and experience.

As you'll have seen from many of the activities, they are there to offer ways for you to develop your criticality on common perceptions and analyse these in a way which will enable you to identify areas of improvement. Many of these activities follow a similar approach to that used in cognitive behavioural therapy, which is a well-known psychology technique used to treat unhelpful thoughts and the influence these have on behaviour and emotion. Although the approaches here aren't usually trying to overcome unhelpful thoughts, they are building more effective thought processes based on a wide range of external influences. The variety of this information, which is constantly reviewed and questioned over the long-term as part of the course, creates the breadth and depth of knowledge which can then be used in future perceptive thinking and in the skill of quickly developing practical approaches to problems.

Key takeaway points – content overview:

- There are a range of ways business schools aim to embed the knowledge and skills developed during an MBA, which can include the following methods:
    - Reading (journal articles, book extracts, case studies, news articles, industry papers) and watching videos (such as TED talks and YouTube videos).

- - - This aims to help you to understand the concepts and support discussion.
  - Interactive learning (lectures, industry talks and visits, seminars, workshops, interviews, personal and group practical activities, presentations and dedicated self-reflection)
    - This aims to help you to embed learnings through engagement with the material and the cohort.
  - Networking, which naturally occurs throughout these activities, will provide an opportunity for you to be able to seek out individuals you may want to engage with throughout your course.
- The content overview presented here is an example and should give you a feel for how you might spend your time in real terms and help you to understand if this is something you both want to do and would also benefit from.

6.2 Specialisms and your expectations

MBAs are supposed to be generalist rather than specialist and this is partly what gives them value, due to the breadth of knowledge gained. With this in mind, it's worth putting thought into what value you might get from any MBAs that offer specialisms, whether this is in finance, technology, entrepreneurship or whatever else it might be. Part of this might be a way for the business school to differentiate itself and attract higher calibre or more candidates. Your decision may be situation and course specific but there often isn't time in an MBA to truly specialise in any depth and breadth and MBAs offering this are often doing it as a marketing tactic.

If you're thinking about doing a specialised MBA, this isn't necessarily always a bad idea. However, it's worth considering whether an MBA is the right way to specialise in that particular field. As an example, if you're considering something like a finance specialism, the trouble often becomes that the specialism doesn't mean anything in this profession beyond a very basic standard equivalent to a bottom tier qualification. As for entrepreneurship, you don't really need an MBA to be an entrepreneur. Many business schools use this to focus on the analysis of entrepreneurship, rather than teaching you how to be one in a practical sense.

Similarly, some MBA courses offer optional modules in project management. For modules such as this, which offer insight into a very common skill, it's worth considering whether the missed opportunity of not doing other modules will be worth spending the time on this generic and common area. Project management can often be more effectively learned through other means, such as specific project management qualifications. These specific qualifications will also almost certainly hold more weight than a module within an MBA when applying for jobs which often require the project management qualifications as prerequisites anyway. The fact you did a module on this within an MBA may not get you through the initial screening exercise if a specific project management qualification is one of the requirements.

Again, doing technology or data as a specialism follows a similar train of thought. However, it's worth looking into exactly what the business school focuses on in slightly different specialisms such as these. As the time you have on your MBA is very limited to go into much depth due to the amount of material covered, it might be that the focus of these modules may actually be worthwhile. For example, regarding data specialisms or optional modules, you're unlikely to come out knowing how to code, but if it gives you enough of an understanding to be able to engage meaningfully with people who can code, it might be worthwhile if that's something that could be useful in your career, such as leading a department which includes or interacts with coders.

The same logic would apply for more unique or emerging specialisms but for these it might be worth considering if there is a way you can get a better insight by exploring your opportunities outside of the MBA, either professionally or vocationally. For anything very specific, we can revisit the myth: you will become an expert in business. In this myth, we mentioned that specific specialisms often rely on the input of a single professor which can be risky for students if the module chooses to go into depth rather than covering the topic in a broad way. The reason this presents risk is you will be reliant on how good that specific professor is. If they're balanced and great at teaching, it could be a risk worth taking but if not, you could be left with a biased and difficult module that is of little use in the practical world.

Although there are practical limitations on the benefit an MBA with specialism will bring you, one of the ways they can be used is to add another element to your halo effect. For example, if you're targeting a move into a specific industry and you're able to present the fact you hold an MBA with a specialism in this field, it may just support your suitability that little bit more. Although it likely won't be worth much on its own in isolation, the sum of the parts of your application will be worth more than the components and a specialism is one way of drawing attention to your commitment and understanding of an area.

Key takeaway points – specialisms and your expectations:

- Evaluate how you would be able to realistically use an MBA with specialism. How respected would this be compared to an industry qualification that can be gained outside of the MBA?
- Look into the details of the specialist modules to understand the topics covered and whether this might provide a broad understanding of the area or a deep understanding of a specific topic within the specialist area. This will help you gauge whether choosing this route will be aligned to your goals.

- Explore whether an MBA with a particular specialism could be used to enhance your halo effect.

Chapter Seven

How to Increase Your Chances of Getting Good Marks

On a fundamental level, being willing to do more than others are prepared to do will help you to secure good marks. As a principle used generally, this will also help you achieve more, open and explore more opportunities and excel in your priorities. It will require your energy and commitment but is highly recommended as a strategy for success. Aside from this general principle which you can adopt and apply to your MBA and career journey, there are specific ways you can achieve good marks which we'll explore in the following sections.

7.1 Criticality

Your ability to demonstrate critical thought underpins the MBA experience and is your key to unlocking marks. This skill can, over time, make MBA cohorts overly critical and sometimes appear pessimistic – just wait until you're asked for feedback on your course about modules or experiences and you will quickly witness this phenomenon! However, it is this criticality that will allow you to develop the skill of being able to spot where things might not be working and identify how they can be improved, based on evidence and taking emotion mostly out of the equation.

Taking a critical approach, you will need to assess the evidence and consistently challenge your own beliefs and assumptions – this is essential in the MBA experience. We mentioned in the myth 'getting an MBA will automatically increase your leadership skills', that not being truly open to new attitudes and beliefs can harm your leadership skill development, but this applies to all of your skills and understanding. You absolutely must be open to the views and concepts presented by others in order to challenge your own assumptions but in doing so, you need to dig deeper into understanding where those concepts came from and why others hold the views they do. This analysis will help you to demonstrate critical thought, as once you understand the motives and rationale of others, you can begin to deconstruct their logic and question it in light of other evidence and the context of their motives.

In your assessments, it is this deconstructing of a challenge and the associated concepts that allow you to holistically analyse complex situations. Through this analysis, a crucial skill lies in the ability to see the main themes that might influence outcomes. This is a highly sought-after skill in business, as the ability to get to the root of a complex problem and quickly and holistically address it, in a way that prevents its reoccurrence and embeds change through the team, can be the difference between an effective leader and a mediocre one.

This skill can be demonstrated in a variety of ways throughout your assessments and by repeating this during the MBA you will come out of the other end with an ability to do this relatively automatically. You may have previously already been able to demonstrate this capability, but the benefit of the MBA is that it exposes you to a significant range of concepts and views, which should expand your potential solutions to complex issues, as well as making your solutions more balanced and holistic. Here are some quick ways you can demonstrate criticality:

- Seek to analyse the motives of others to understand if their rationale was biased. For example, was a specific area of research conducted in a way that lent itself to those conclusions? Or in case studies, why might a bad or a good management situation have come about as a result of the personal motivations of those involved?
- When analysing decisions, what are the knock-on impacts for teams as a result of decisions? What is the likely effect on culture? How might the team culture cause resistance to, or positively impact, the effectiveness of a proposed change?
- When analysing conceptual models, how do these compare and contrast with models that look to address similar areas? Are there areas of one

model which are missed or expanded on in similar frameworks? Could a better model be created by combining two or more existing approaches? To truly demonstrate this engagement, you can even map out a proposed adaptation of existing models in your assessment, which goes above and beyond what would often be expected.

- When analysing strategy, is the strategy aligned throughout the organisation? Are there parts of the organisation that do not align or seem to contradict the strategy? Why might this be?
- When analysing data, was there a chance of bias in the way it was collected? What are the characteristics of the data and are the right analysis and presentation tools being used for the type of data you're working with?

These are just some aspects of just a few areas you will be able to show criticality in, but these should give you a flavour of the types of aspects you should be aiming to compare and contrast. Every situation will be unique and require a unique analysis. The more you engage with others on your course, professors and those in your network who might work in your current or future target industry on this topic, the more holistic a view you will likely be able to make.

Many real-world business problems are complex in nature and present many variables. Effective leaders are able to navigate through the uncertainty, in some part, through the use of assumptions based on the evidence available. When that evidence changes, the ability to quickly review and adapt a strategy as needed is a skill that few in middle-management appear to master, with this being one of the softer skills an MBA aims to teach.

Key takeaway points – criticality:

- To get the most from the MBA and help unlock higher marks, you should look to consistently assess new evidence and situations, using these insights to challenge your existing assumptions and beliefs.
- Understanding the motives and rationale of others will allow you to deconstruct their logic and question it in light of other evidence and the context of their motives. Demonstrating this thought process will help show your criticality.
- Through critical analysis, you can develop the highly sought-after skill of getting to the root cause of a complex problem and implementing mitigating actions to address the issue, preventing reoccurrence and embedding change through your team.

7.2 Tutor bias

This is a controversial topic but due to the nature of your assignments, they often won't be marked anonymously even if there are anonymous methods of submission. One of the ways this can happen is if you're applying your assignments to specific businesses, there is usually some discussion on scope between students and professors. Alternatively, the professor may know that you are in contact or involved with a specific company covered in your assignment, through mention of them in class discussions and your examples. Assignments are often supposed to be anonymous as per standard university practice and would normally be in most undergraduate degrees, but for various reasons this anonymity often doesn't materialise in MBAs. Your professors and the university would always strongly deny it but it's only natural for there to be a risk of some personal bias when anonymity is taken away.

If your professor prefers a particular theory or approach, then it may be received more favourably if you incorporate these theories and approaches into your work. However, the success of approaches such as this is so dependent on the people and academic components involved that using bias to your advantage can't and shouldn't be relied on as something to help you. Generally, it's better to be respectful but justified with your views and contribute to classes as best you can when it's appropriate and when you can add value. If any positive results come from this approach, it wouldn't have been artificially or purposely cultivated through the manipulation of bias, which otherwise might be viewed as pretty unethical behaviour.

Key takeaway points – tutor bias:

- Anonymity in marking is often very difficult to achieve due to the nature of MBA course assessments, leading to some risk of bias.
- Trying to use bias to your advantage is not something that often can or indeed should be relied on as something to help you. Your best approach is to be respectful and justified with your views, contributing to classes where you can add value. If positive results come from this approach, then you will not have artificially cultivated it, which may be viewed as unethical behaviour.

7.3 Collaboration

Assessments involving team activities can present difficulties even if you're normally great at working with people. Due to the usually international nature of MBAs, you will typically find yourself on a team which has people from several cultural backgrounds. For online courses, your peers may also be across several time zones. This is then combined with those people generally wanting to prove themselves as capable and, depending on their motivations, may want to impress the professor and stand out from the team for some other reason, through demonstrating leadership or whatever it might be. Although this might sound like an exaggeration and an unrealistic scenario, it does happen. In full-time courses where participation is marked, this situation can be intensified. Your experience will often come down to what personalities are on your team, but you will have to quickly work out a way of effectively collaborating with others to deliver something meaningful for the assessment.

There is also the risk that someone can complain that not all on the team provided a comparable input, which can sometimes be done through a specific process enabling people to confidentially disclose where they feel this has occurred. This is intended to discourage some in the team from relying on the work of others and benefiting from the marks where they may have put little effort into the process. Your best approach in overcoming the risk of someone making this complaint about you is to not shy away from work and be responsive when you might be working remotely with your team or if the work extends over more than a few days. If you delay responding for too long, the lack of responsiveness may prompt another team member to take on the work you were originally allocated to do, resulting in a feeling of unfairness in the team. Again, this might seem unlikely but, it does happen and when deadlines are tight and pressure is high, many people's sense of reasonableness and tolerance for slower responses may be reduced.

Despite the challenges associated with a multi-cultural group representing a diverse range of professional backgrounds working under tight deadlines, the diversity created through the team can be especially beneficial. The range of approaches and perspectives put forward by the group can help you develop a stronger understanding of the topic whilst also developing a more holistic output for the assessment. Diversity is a proven driver of innovation and you can use this to your advantage in trying to take an original approach to solving problems or addressing challenges. Similarly, as your team will likely have distinct strengths, it's worth considering how you can make the most of your individual strengths to optimise your time and secure the highest marks possible.

From a cultural point of view, tailoring your approach to individual team members may help you get the best from your team. Most MBA courses cover techniques for this within management and leadership modules but if you haven't covered the topic by the time you have your team assessments, it's worth doing some initial research into general cultural preferences and how they may differ. You can then tailor your actions and approaches according to your insights to help minimise potential challenges, maximise the effectiveness of the team and as a result, increase the chance of securing higher marks.

Although most sources advising on cultural considerations will be generalisations, which may not always apply to individuals, it is still worth bearing them in mind. These considerations can be useful in helping you to spot cues which may confirm these generalisations apply to varying degrees in the people you meet. For example, some cultures may prefer a more emotional as opposed to a measured interaction, may prioritise hierarchy to varying degrees, may be more or less individualistic and may prioritise success differently. There are many different characteristics that can differ from person to person but being aware of these potential areas of variation can give you an advantage in understanding why people behave in the ways they do and how you can navigate around potential resistance to ideas or ways of working. Researching Hofstede's cultural dimensions may be a good way to build some initial knowledge of this before you need to work in teams.

Key takeaway points – collaboration:

- Assignments involving team activities as part of the assessment can provide challenge due to the professional and cultural diversity found on MBA cohorts, tight deadlines and need for individuals to deliver an equal input to the overall group output.
- Your ability to quickly gauge how best to work with your team and tailor your approach based on this is a key strength to unlocking higher marks, through the ability to reduce potential conflict and resistance and aligning the team towards the common goal of delivering the best potential output.
- Most MBA courses will cover cultural diversity and techniques for maximising success in diverse teams. If you haven't covered this before any team assessments, researching Hofstede's cultural dimensions can give you a good level of understanding and awareness of some common

cultural differences that you can consider in your approach with your team.
- By understanding that cultural and personal differences can occur within teams, you can tailor your actions and approach to help minimise potential challenges, maximise the effectiveness of the team and as a result, increase the chance of securing higher marks.

7.4 Methods of assessment

As we covered briefly in Chapter Four when we discussed the pros and cons of the different modes of study, some modes of study and modules will likely have different methods of assessment. These may offer some opportunities to secure comparatively easier marks. Although in theory this shouldn't happen, it was known on my own course that the modules offering a more intensive experience were often the ones you were likely to score higher marks in. These included modules that included trips to leading businesses, with intensity being brought in through the learning and assessment processes.

The reason behind this varied between modules but generally, the more intensive the module, the more this was taken into account in the marking and the closer you were to both the course material and the professors, resulting in you gaining a better understanding of what they were looking for. Professors are often very aware that students want to achieve the highest marks possible and many students on my specific course were willing to ask some especially direct questions of the professors on what would and wouldn't secure high marks. For some professors, the continued pressure of these direct questions did make them give away some great hints and tips. If you keep listening to all of these insights throughout your module, by the end you should be able to build a pretty good picture of exactly what they are and aren't looking for in your assessment.

My personal approach to this, which worked very well for me, was to note down these hints and tips as the module progressed. By the end of the module, this produced a list of ways to secure high marks in that particular assessment for that specific professor. Twinned with the marking criteria, this can then be used as a checklist for your assignment to ensure your work will meet the highest expectations that have been shared with you. Clearly, on top of this you will need to look at the assessment itself in addition to this checklist, but it can be a good start.

A great way to consider what else you can do to achieve high marks is by combining this checklist approach with the principle we started Chapter Seven with: be willing to do more than others are willing to do. This can be particularly effective when applied to the criticality you show, which can be thought about in the context of the prompts we covered earlier in the criticality section. In essence, how can you show original critical thought by analysing a problem in a way that others may not have thought of, going above and beyond what they are willing to do?

A key to understanding the module by module marking situation is through speaking with recent alumni and if you're looking at multi-year MBA courses, those in the year above your current year or who have already completed that specific module. These are critical contacts to make and, in some universities where modules are running on a rotational basis with multiple intakes per year, MBA students from different intakes may attend the same modules. This can offer opportunities to share knowledge, best approaches across the modules and how others may have secured high marks.

The different methods of assessment, whether these are short or extended assignments, exams, individual and group presentations, and participation in classes, allow you to play to your strengths where securing the highest marks possible is your primary goal. If you know a strength of yours is academic writing, you'll want to choose optional modules that are geared more towards this. Similarly, if you're great at working with people and are more of an extrovert, you might find group presentations to be an area you'll excel at and subsequently reap the rewards in marks awarded.

Most of the time, method of assessment isn't likely to be a priority in your module selection. However, if by the time you come to choose your elective modules you're bordering between grade boundaries, you may want to consider if securing that higher grade is likely to give you any advantage. This may be particularly helpful in cultivating your halo effect, but will need to be considered against any modules that you really want to take, but you don't think you would do as comparatively well in.

Key takeaway points – methods of assessment:

- Modules with a more intensive learning experience and method of assessment may offer the opportunity to secure higher marks as you will be closer to the material, cohort and professors and may be able to build a greater understanding of the expectations.
- Direct questions to professors on assessment requirements may provide insights into how higher marks may be secured. By keeping a note of these throughout the module, you can build a checklist of requirements for your assessment. This can be used in parallel with the mark scheme and your ability to go above and beyond requirements, particularly in your criticality.
- Recent alumni, students in the year above (if you're in a multi-year MBA) and those who may have already completed modules if they are running on a rotational basis can be great sources of information and learning on how to secure high marks.
- Different methods of assessment offering more or less likely ways to secure higher marks for you as an individual can allow you to play to your

strengths where securing high marks is your priority.

7.5 Effort versus goals

As we alluded to in the methods of assessment section, there is a choice you should make about how much effort you are able and willing to put into the MBA as a whole in the context of your goals and what you want to achieve from the experience. For example, if you're already well-established in your career, have been working for 15 years, but need the MBA on your CV to progress to the next career level, you're unlikely to want to put in as much effort to getting high marks in every assignment. Alternatively, if you're transitioning into business from a non-business background, you're a lot more likely to want to prove yourself in the content of the course and properly understand the basics. Securing high marks can be a great way of building your confidence initially and proving your competence to others, as you are able to use this as another way to build your halo effect.

It is this effort versus goals decision that is worth thinking about both before and during the course and can help in prioritising your commitments alongside the MBA. This is particularly relevant if you're studying part-time or online but can also apply if you want to maintain specific commitments outside of a full-time MBA. However, it's more likely that if you're pursuing a full-time MBA, it's because your goals rely heavily on you doing well throughout the MBA and so you may have already started down the path that naturally leads to you putting in the most effort you possibly can.

You will find that although no MBA course is easy, for most programmes, if you do the reading, contribute to the classes and absorb and engage with the material, you will be unlikely to fail. This leniency also holds true regarding the standard of writing in written assessments, with slightly poor writing not necessarily always resulting in very poor marks. This is because the point of an MBA isn't academic writing, but the ability to apply concepts to real-world problems and think critically. This emphasis is clearly different to that of a traditional university experience and in the case of an MBA, helps the stereotypical student as a busy professional interested in how they can apply concepts to improve their business, rather than the nuances of writing something that could be published as a journal article.

Although this leniency is shown by some universities, the extent will vary depending on the institution and the standards they work to. Mark schemes will include writing, grammar and referencing as part of the assessment, but as long as you can successfully convey your reasoning and messages you will generally be fine, as this is where the majority of marks are awarded. The level of tolerance for errors in your writing may depend on how internationally diverse the cohort is, as where diversity is higher, concessions may be made based on the need to use a common language in assessments. Despite the potential leniency in this area, it's also worth noting that if you are able to perfect your writing style, grammar and your referencing to be as close to 100% accurate as possible, you may be more likely to secure high marks due to the overall positive perception this is likely to give the professor. Likewise, if the work is poorly written, full of grammatical errors and the referencing has been incorrectly done according to the standards expected, this may be the difference between passing or failing, or only just passing and receiving a merit. A poor standard of writing can make the work more difficult to mark for someone assessing the work, which may result in a less favourable mark if the message you're trying to convey is lost in translation.

Ultimately, higher marks are there for those who want to put in the effort and time to achieving them but attaining high marks will often take considerably more effort than it would take to obtain an MBA at a pass level. Effort required to achieve a pass will vary significantly from person to person, depending on your natural abilities and experience. It is likely that you won't be able to gauge your natural abilities and how these compare with the expectations required until after your first assessment. To make this even harder to judge, your aptitude can also differ from module to module. Understanding this variation alongside your strengths and weaknesses can help you to be dynamic in the amount of effort you put into the different modules as the course progresses and help you in achieving your overall goals.

Most employers don't ask potential candidates for their post-graduate degree grades, but as more and more people secure advanced degrees, high marks can be used as a distinguishing factor and can help to support your halo effect. If you're targeting highly competitive industries, this may be a benefit to you. However, if you're simply wanting to progress your career beyond where you are now, or if MBAs aren't commonplace in your industry, the grading won't be a major factor. I've witnessed first-hand from countless others in my own cohort how much this realisation has reduced the pressure on them, when they have initially struggled with workload but were content with achieving an MBA at a pass level and so were able to invest comparatively less effort into the process to align with their goals. Going into the experience with clear expectations, aligned to your goals, will help to reduce the pressure on you if you're happy with a pass or alternatively help justify why you put in the effort you do if you want to achieve a merit or distinction.

Key takeaway points – effort versus goals:

- Thinking about the MBA in the context of your non-MBA commitments, priorities, goals and what you want or need to achieve from the experience will help you work out how much effort you're able and willing to invest in the course.
- Effort required to pass will depend on your natural abilities, experience and your aptitude on specific modules. You will likely only be able to judge what this means for you and the effort you will need to put in to pass once you have been through the

first module. Once you understand this, you may be able to tailor the effort you invest module by module, to achieve the marks aligned with your goals and priorities.
- Not targeting high marks if you don't need to can take considerable pressure away from the experience. Most employers will not ask for grades at a post-graduate level, but high grades can be used to enhance your halo effect.
- Higher marks are there for those who want to put in the effort and time to achieving them but achieving high marks will likely take considerably more effort than it would take to achieve an MBA at a pass level.

Chapter Eight

Maximising Your Opportunities Before, During and After Your MBA

This book has explored a variety of ways you can maximise your experiences and opportunities throughout your MBA journey. This ranges from understanding your needs and overcoming initial challenges to considering the characteristics of each business school and method of study. Thought needs to be given as to the right amount of effort you should invest in each aspect of your experience, in relation to your goals during the MBA. As part of this, you should also consider how you can best manage both internal and external stakeholders throughout your entire end-to-end MBA experience to make the most of your potential options. Combined together, the areas covered so far provide high-impact areas you need to consider and work through to ensure you get the most out of your MBA and in doing so, maximise your opportunities.

This section will summarise and recapture some of the essential aspects you should be considering in the order of when you may want to think about them. Although some of this is a more focused version of the content covered, many topics have additional aspects to make sure you're clear on how these characteristics can be used to maximise your opportunities. In doing this, it's worth thinking as broad as possible to understand whether any of these areas present prospects for you to improve on your personal and professional situation. Every set of individual circumstances are unique with distinct opportunities and risks which all need to be factored in. With an open mindset, think about what actions would help enable you to increase your value to other people and businesses in the job market. Your ability to improve your own value offering and brand is fundamental to improving your own opportunities. Many of these areas of potential increased value can be applied broadly as principles to work through when considering your career development, even if you decide an MBA isn't necessarily for you.

8.1 Before your MBA

Understand what you are looking for and what you want to achieve

A key starting point you need to consider is what you are looking for and what you want to achieve, thinking specifically around the below questions:

- What type of experience are you searching for and what are you hoping to gain from an MBA?

- Is an MBA the way you will most effectively achieve what you are hoping to achieve?
    - What have you based this assumption on?
    - Is there clear evidence to support your assumption?
    - You may be able to confirm this through speaking with others in your targeted career path or industry, but in doing so, be aware of any potential bias on both their part and yours.
- What characteristics of a business school are most important for you in helping to achieve your goals?
    - How does your research support this?
    - How well do the characteristics of the business school fit with your own personal situation and your preferences?
- What aspects of an MBA education are you willing to compromise on and what is essential?
    - Would you compromise by choosing a less preferred mode of study for you, if this allows you to complete an MBA earlier in your career?
    - Would you be willing to compromise on the prestige of a business school if it might be more likely to help you secure contacts in a specific industry you may be targeting?
- Which MBA course, business school and mode of study is likely to give you the best potential return on investment for your time and money?

- - Is this return on investment aligned to your goals and the resources you have available to you or are you seeking, or need to seek, something else?
- Is there a level of risk in your approach and are you, and anyone else involved in the decision, able and willing to take this risk?
  - - If your targeted MBA course relies on you taking on large amounts of debt or moving your family, are they truly aligned with what you're looking to achieve and what it will take to make it a success? Do they understand the commitment required from you in terms of time?

This list is not exhaustive but having clarity on these sorts of questions in your own mind will help you to understand which business schools would match with your goals and subsequently focus your effort in researching for and completing applications. In the early stages of your potential MBA journey, it goes without saying that you should do the necessary research to make sure you understand what it is you truly want to achieve. Once you understand what your ultimate goals are, your research will help you map out a realistic path of how to get there and how an MBA fits into this journey.

This clarity on your purpose and objectives will greatly help you to communicate this throughout your application to a potential business school, who will be looking to understand your drive and reasoning for pursuing an MBA. If a business school doesn't fit with your criteria, it will likely be harder to tailor your application in a convincing way and may reduce your chances of a successful application. Your personal fit with a potential university works on both your expectations of the business school and the university's expectations of you as a potential candidate. The clarity you develop here will also help in any communication you need to provide to your employer, those potentially providing references as well as any other stakeholders along your journey.

Understand any limitations and where you may need to reduce or overcome these

Limitations can come in many forms and your research will help uncover where these may present any risks for your application. These might be presented in the following areas:

- Employer support and references.
- Funding.
- MBA course requirements, including the below key criteria:
    - Professional experience.
    - Academic qualifications.
    - Admissions tests.
    - English proficiency.
- Your own confidence in your abilities.
- Available time.

We'll cover each of these in turn to provide some ways you can overcome these potential challenges.

- **Secure employer support and references**

At the outset of your MBA journey, you should explore how willing to support your professional network are, particularly those who may act as employer and professional references. University requirements can differ and although many MBA courses will state a required reference from your current employer, there may be flexibility in this depending on your circumstances. Don't let this requirement put you off if this is proving particularly challenging.

A reference could come from your current employer, a recent employer, or business contact such as a key supplier or buyer. As we covered in Chapter Two, this can provide challenges which are often heavily influenced by the perception and expectations of those you're asking. When seeking a potential referee, think about their level of seniority and those who are likely to provide you with the best possible reference. You want to try and find the most senior person you can who will provide the strongest reference, with the result being the most favourable portrayal of you and your potential to the business school. You will need to gauge the level of willingness of this referee, whether it's your line manager or someone else, and bring them along with you on your journey by involving them in the process and seeking their counsel, helping them to become invested in your success. If you aren't asking your line manager for a reference, depending on the personal characteristics of those involved, you may need to play this very carefully so that you don't create unnecessary tension.

This same principle applies not just for references, but for any other employer support including time off and monetary contributions. This is likely to be best approached as early as possible in your journey and in a soft manner. One way you can do this is by positioning your intentions as wanting to develop yourself and through doing this, enable you to bring increased value to your company through your new enhanced capabilities. If you can quantify the benefits the company is likely to see as a result of your MBA experience, this can help in making your goal tangible and gaining the commitment you need. If you come across any pushback when gauging potential commitment or raising your request, it's good to try to understand the reasons behind this to identify how you might best overcome it. You may identify ways around this over a period of time or, worst-case scenario, choose to pursue the MBA without the support of your employer. There may be several ways you can achieve an MBA, with all options worth considering in the context of your priorities and any risks each option may present.

- <u>Secure funding</u>

As we covered in Chapter Five, cost and debt are understandably the main reason people don't pursue MBAs. There are significant considerations for you on these topics, but there may also be a few options open to you:

- Employer full funding.
- Employer part funding.

- - Both of the above may involve repayment terms if you leave the company.
- Personal full funding.
- Personal part funding.
  - Both of these subsequent options may involve using savings or taking on personal debt through personal or government-based loans.
- Scholarship full funding.
- Scholarship part funding.
  - These final two options can exist in various forms and come from various sources within, and external to, the university.

Both employer and personal funding may have opportunity costs associated with them, in that there may be other opportunities that you would forego in using that opportunity, savings, or ability to take on debt. This needs to be compared against the benefit of an MBA in your situation and whether you are happy to sacrifice the alternatives in pursuit of the MBA. Doing an MBA will usually present some sort of risk. One of the ways you need to evaluate this is from a financial perspective in the context of what opportunities and potential return it may provide you and what the likelihood of these are.

The level of funding required and how much the specific MBA you're targeting will cost you is fundamentally linked to your priorities and goals. The cost of the MBA itself can vary significantly depending on university, location and mode of study. Similarly, the mode of study will dictate your need to take time out of employment and any lost earnings which might result from this. However, if, for example, your research suggests the MBA you are looking to complete would help you achieve your goals, and if these are to increase salary by moving industries or through progression, this may help alleviate some of the concern of the initial outlay and risk by setting out a clear potential return on your investment.

Despite the opportunity MBAs can present for career progression and maximising your opportunities, as we have mentioned, there is no denying that they often present a risk that you will need to take in order to reap the potential rewards. This ability to take a risk based on your individual circumstances should also form a key part of your assessment, including which MBA courses and modes of study you target. As part of this risk assessment, it is also worth evaluating the timing of your MBA journey and how you can maximise your opportunities by using this timing to help in your career trajectory. By planning to complete your MBA at a point that makes sense for you in your career, you can use the experience to expand further in your current role, progress into a more senior role or transition into a different role. Irrelevant of when you pursue the MBA, it is your open mindset and use of it in building your halo effect, as well as your hard and soft skills, that will support the maximisation of opportunities.

- Positioning yourself against MBA course requirements

Although your professional experience and academic qualifications go hand in hand within your application, one can be presented with more emphasis than the other to maximise your strengths and minimise your weaknesses. As we covered in Chapter Two on developing an effective CV, strengths in either one of these areas can be used to enhance your halo effect. Generally, with MBA applications, weaknesses in academic qualifications can be overcome by strong professional experience.

Limitations in English proficiency can be overcome by taking tests to demonstrate this, ahead of time and as part of the application, or by demonstrating examples of your use of English in professional or personal settings. Internationally focused schools will understand varying levels of capability although a standard level of competence is expected. This not only ensures teaching will be effective but also that you can get the most from the experience. Particularly on courses where participation is graded, poor English proficiency can really prevent marks from being achieved.

A wealth of information is available online for the admissions tests that universities use as standard and the general advice is to make sure you are achieving the scores required reliably on mock tests wherever possible before sitting the real thing. These are a tick box exercise but without them, you may fall at the first hurdle.

- <u>Having confidence in your abilities</u>

Some people struggle to maintain confidence in their own abilities throughout their MBA journey, which can have a comparatively large detrimental impact during the initial stages. It is not the time to be modest during the application process and as many people naturally are, either due to individual or cultural characteristics, this can provide an area of challenge. It may be uncomfortable at first, but you often need to move out of your comfort zone in order to grow. Having a trusted and supportive friend, colleague, family member or partner to act as a sounding board can help to occasionally reassure you. However, it is important to remember that a lot of people will have similar self-doubting thoughts, no matter how confident they appear. It is often the ability to conceal this self-doubt that opens up your ability to put yourself out there and subsequently benefit from opportunities.

- <u>Committing the necessary time</u>

Many people struggle to find the time to balance the wide range of demands and deadlines that occur throughout the MBA experience, with these starting from the very beginning of the journey. There will be many peaks in these demands over time, which will need to be worked through and overcome. Taking a segmented and disciplined approach to time management is one fundamental way this can be achieved. Even when beginning your journey whilst researching your options, allocating set regular time to do this as part of a routine can help in beginning to form the good habit of having a balance in your priorities and committing to them.

Many people pursuing an MBA have families and other commitments and it goes without saying that these are important priorities that need to be balanced fairly and appropriately. Getting the support of those in your life and having a common understanding of the new commitment you face is a fundamental part of striking this balance during the time you'll be working towards your MBA.

Now that we've revisited some of the potentially limiting challenges you might face and how you can overcome these, we'll return to the things you can explore before your MBA to maximise your career opportunities.

Understand your strengths

Your application isn't the time to be modest about your achievements and strengths. It's a time to emphasise to the business school why you're different, how you have what it takes to succeed and how you can bring significant value to the cohort. Standing out from the crowd of other MBA applicants is your main focus and there are some things you might want to consider in doing this:

- How have your abilities resulted in high-impact results for you or those around you? What were these high-impact results?

- Have you been able to overcome significant personal or professional setbacks, learning from these to further improve yourself or others?
- How do your strengths and abilities differ to that of others and why does this make you suited to be an MBA candidate at that specific business school? Have you seen opportunities where others haven't? Have you been able to overcome issues that others have struggled with? If so, how did you effectively manage this to create value, deliver impact and influence others? If you had an MBA, how might you be able to take this capability one step further and achieve even greater things?
- How do your examples demonstrate your ambition and determination to succeed?
- What did these experiences teach you about yourself and how would they benefit the business school?

Understanding your strengths won't just help you sell yourself as a great prospective student to the business school but will also help articulate your worth more effectively to your employer. It can be easy to forget your employer or potential employers in the goal to secure an MBA but they are as important, if not more so, in maximising your opportunities. The MBA in and of itself is not worth anything – it is how you apply the learnings from the whole experience to your situation that will deliver benefits to you. These learnings aren't just developed during the course but begin to be formed as early as this initial point in starting your journey towards applying.

When working through your application, you will start to develop your skills of portraying your knowledge and experience in a more refined way and it is your ability to communicate this effectively that will be one aspect in helping you to progress your career.

Research what the business school specific values are

Business school values and how visible these are can vary from school to school but are worth spending some dedicated time researching. In doing this, you can ensure they align with your own values and also consider how they can be factored into your application, through demonstrating your alignment with them. They should be available by looking through the course material, watching alumni and staff interviews which are often available online as well as looking at the university website. In today's world of ethics playing an increasing part in business, it's important that you position yourself with this in mind as it will be expected that you operate with integrity. If there is any way you can work examples of where you held yourself or others accountable for their actions into your application, you can use this to convey your commitment to doing the right thing.

Tailor and develop your CV, cover letter and application

Invest the time developing and tailoring your CV to be the best it can be in both content and structure. This should be tailored to the individual university for each of your applications. By continuing to develop your CV, as your experience and skills progress, you will also benefit from having a more refined CV immediately following the MBA in your likely subsequent job search. Adopting the four-step approach for maximum impact (covered in Chapter Two) will help to outline your work experience in an easy to understand and relatable way. Throughout your CV you want to use the halo effect to your advantage by drawing attention to your strongest, highest impact and most impressive achievements first.

One of the best ways you can develop your CV is through more gradual development. Keep coming back to your CV with fresh eyes to minimise the chance of errors and incrementally improve content, visual appeal and structure. In doing this, you will have more chance of spotting any errors in spelling and grammar, which can be hard to spot when you become accustomed with a piece of your own writing. To further reduce the risk of errors, you can ask a trusted, competent and diligent friend, colleague or family member who may be willing to help check your work.

Engage with your internal network

The internal network presented through your previous or current employer presents a significant area of opportunity in any attempt to use an MBA to further your career and compensation. From the point you begin to investigate who may be appropriate to secure a reference from, you will be engaging with these stakeholders and it will be beneficial to keep them informed of your application progress and any developments in the options available to you. By also keeping colleagues informed about your journey from the very start, you may help to alleviate potential future resistance once you begin to attempt to implement any learnings from the course and need their support.

Throughout your MBA journey, it is worth continuing to be aware of your wider internal network, which may include family and friends as well as acquaintances from any hobbies you may have, such as societies, sports or charity work. This may not only provide opportunities for you but may also allow you to provide opportunities or advice for others.

Engage with your external network

Your external network is what people usually refer to when they highlight the benefit of networking on MBA courses. Although the business school may support you in helping to develop this by providing opportunities such as networking events, you need to put in the work to get the most out of external interactions and subsequently build your reputation.

You can explore your MBA cohort network even before you start the MBA – LinkedIn is a great place to get to know your future cohort and hit the ground running. Your reputation within your cohort whilst on the MBA can help you secure higher marks, through enhancing your interactions with others on material during the course. To maximise the chance of developing a strong network, using the time before your MBA is a great way to start to establish these initial relationships.

Industry networks can be a great way to raise your profile and gain valuable insights before you start your MBA and throughout your journey. These may be formal or informal networks you can connect with through existing representatives in your company or through platforms such as LinkedIn. Consultancy firms can also hold forums for representatives of competitors within industries to discuss challenging topics. These offer a great way to network with your counterparts in other companies, which can be particularly beneficial as you embark on your MBA experience as it will present increasing opportunities to share and gain crucial insights.

8.2 During your MBA

MBA content is frequently centred around strategy. If this interests you, being visibly enthusiastic about the development and implementation of this in your own company should create a natural progression towards you taking on more responsibility. If your ambition might not be clear, you may want to specifically make your intentions obvious. You can do this by sharing that you want to take on more responsibility, using your MBA skills and knowledge to progress into a more senior role.

One of the best ways to pursue increases in pay or other benefits is to approach this after you have added specific value or delivered a tangible benefit, which can be highlighted after the event or within a scheduled performance evaluation such as an end of year review. By adding the fact that the MBA skills and experience directly helped you to deliver specific improvements, you may be able to add weight to the fact that you are now a higher calibre employee, with more experience, who should be paid more in order for your compensation to be reflective of your abilities and higher impact on the business.

Balance your time and priorities

Thinking about the MBA in the context of your non-MBA commitments, priorities, goals and what you want or need to achieve from the experience will help you work out how much effort you're able and willing to invest in the course. Effort and time required to pass will depend highly on your natural abilities, experience and your aptitude on specific modules. You will likely only be able to judge what this means for you and the effort you will need to put in to pass once you have been through the first module. Once you understand this, you may be able to tailor the effort you invest on a module by module basis, to achieve the marks and experience suited to your goals.

Once you've started the MBA, it's easy to become engulfed with the deadlines and commitments of the course. However, it's worth remembering to continue to prioritise your non-MBA commitments and make sure you keep a tab on how these other areas of your life are faring. This might be your family, partner or friends or your current work if you're on a part-time or online course. This will naturally be easier for some people rather than others, but for some it can be easy to neglect other elements of their life during what is an intensive period of time. Although you will understand the pressures that you're under, this might not always be clear to those around you at the time.

Achieve the highest marks you can

Not targeting high marks if you don't need to can take considerable pressure away from the whole MBA experience. Most employers will not ask for grades at a post-graduate level, but high grades can be used to enhance your halo effect. Higher marks are there for those who want to put in the effort and time to achieving them, but achieving high marks will likely take considerably more effort and time than it would take to achieve an MBA at a pass level.

However, trying the hardest you can (in line with your goals and priorities) will ensure you secure the highest mark you can achieve, rather than the highest in the class. Although your mark in comparison to others might be relevant for your final grade, you as an individual doing the best you can is important in understanding what your current capabilities actually are. It might not be a realistic goal to aim to be top of the class in every module if your current strengths do not lie in MBA assignments!

As we covered in Chapter Seven, on a fundamental level, being willing to do more than others are willing to do will help you to secure good marks. As a principle used generally, this will also help you achieve more, open and explore more opportunities and excel in your priorities. It will require your energy and commitment, but it is highly recommended as a strategy for success. Aside from this general principle which you can adopt and apply to your MBA and career journey, there are specific ways you can achieve top marks. These were covered in a lot more detail in Chapter Seven, but include your ability to go above and beyond, your criticality, effective collaboration and playing to your strengths in the methods of assessments targeted.

Engage with your internal network

By tailoring your assignments to your organisation or a role you're targeting, you can increase the quality of relationships within your network as well as improving your understanding of the organisation and role. Tailored assignments provide an opportunity to involve stakeholders whilst also showcasing your abilities to those who may have influence over your future career progression and income. This is a win-win scenario as they may derive some insights from having your focus on their business and you benefit by raising your profile, whilst also getting their input on your assignment, increasing the chance of you taking a more holistic and critical approach and producing a higher quality piece of work. By tailoring your assignments, you can also more tangibly demonstrate to your influential stakeholders that there is a clear link between your MBA and improved value to both your personal development and a business.

As well as prospective employers, it's worth ensuring you also don't neglect those in your network who have endorsed company sponsorship for you or were supportive of your application – these people are already invested in your success. There is a chance these stakeholders will have expectations of you whilst you work towards an MBA and following completion, particularly if they include your line manager and any of their superiors. Ensure you remain aligned with their expectations to protect your reputation. You want to make sure they continue to feel that their investment in you was a good choice for the business and reflects well on them.

You have an opportunity to bring as many colleagues along with you as possible. Their support, or lack of it, can make the difference between a successful initiative and a failed one. Make sure you engage with MBA material on gaining the cooperation of others and seek to involve your colleagues in your work and ideas. Asking for advice and input may help provide alternative perspectives whilst also gaining an element of buy-in to your progress.

<u>Engage with your external network</u>

By reaching out to potential contacts in a business you're interested in, you may be able to form suitable relationships within which you can share select aspects of tailored assignments on the company for input and feedback. As with similar opportunities in your internal network, through this, you can increase your visibility whilst also deepening your understanding of the company to support any subsequent job applications.

Having a good reputation within your cohort often encourages others to be more willing to engage with you on ideas and perspectives, which in turn will help to increase your understanding of the material you're covering as well as helping build good working relationships. Having a good reputation during the MBA can pay dividends following the course, when you may look to your cohort to explore potential employment or further networking opportunities.

Staying aware of current industry challenges through industry networks will allow you to add more insight to your course, whilst improving your chances of being able to add value to businesses through applying the content you learn to real-world business problems. You can use your network to deepen your industry trend insights to identify potential areas of added value for you and your business. Through this, you can increase your reputation in your own network as an expert in your field, helping support a transition into a more senior role.

Explore opportunities for post-MBA employment or career advancement

Due to its intensity, your MBA is likely to make it feel as though it speeds up time. From early on in your MBA, you should be thinking about potential career development and exploring opportunities for employment following your MBA. This can be pursued through your entire network – there are no limits to where you may find potential windows of opportunity. This is particularly relevant for full-time MBA courses, with this search for opportunities often being supported by the business school. Career fairs and application openings often happen very early in the academic year so it is important that if you're reliant on securing post-MBA employment, you don't miss these opportunities and are able to make the most you possibly can from them.

8.3 After your MBA

Continue to engage with your internal network

Your internal network can be an important source of providing low risk, easy to access opportunities which makes this group of people key stakeholders for you to keep engaged, even following your MBA. You can do this by continuing to apply MBA concepts to your work and in doing so, continuing to demonstrate your higher-level impact on the business. Tactfully drawing attention to this link between your MBA and the impact you're having where you can, and where it makes sense to, can help support your case to be put forward for new opportunities. Over and above this, giving something back to the business by sharing your learning with other colleagues, as well as contributing to training materials or strategic developments, can be a great way of reinforcing your value to the business.

Following your MBA, bringing thinking from your external network into your internal network can also be a differentiator in the value you bring and also play a part in developing your personal brand. Many senior leaders in business have extensive external networks they can rely on for advice and who they can develop ideas and opportunities with. It is your ability to begin to tap into this as a resource that can accelerate improvements within your own business and your capacity to do this can significantly enhance your reputation.

Continue to engage with your external network

It might be easy to lose contact with some of those in your network but it's worth maintaining contact where it makes sense to do so. As well as the benefits of keeping in touch on a personal level for any friendships you may have developed, your external network can be a great source of opportunities and industry insights. Sharing opportunities that you may have come across, ideas you may be looking for input on and any challenges you may be facing can be a great way to stay in touch and continue to build your relationships.

With new students starting MBA degrees every year, your potential network is continually expanding. This presents continual new opportunities to build new relationships and this is something you can revisit on a regular basis. Similarly, there may have been some on your cohort who you didn't have the chance to interact with much at the time, or didn't share the same industry, but now have more in common with due to changing circumstances. Reaching back out to these people to re-establish a connection can often provide a head start in what can be great relationships, as a result of the shared experience of completing the MBA together.

Revisit your CV

As we previously covered, your best approach to CV development is to continually review and refine it. As well as tailoring the CV to each individual role, you can maintain a more generic template that can act as a core version, to be amended as needed for each role. Much of the wording in your examples can be consistent through your tailored versions as these will have been refined many times and so should be very effective in communicating your message.

Many universities continue to offer career and CV support following graduation and it can be useful to take advantage of any CV support services available. One of the downsides of regularly reviewing your CV is you may find it difficult to take a step back and spot something obvious that could be changed in a simple way for a much bigger overall effect. By having a professional and fresh pair of eyes review it, you can often take your CV to the next level.

Revisiting your CV towards both the end and following your MBA will allow you to apply your learnings and enhanced communication skills to the document, improving it even further. As you will have also been putting your MBA learnings into practice, this can also be an opportunity to include these successes into your CV, highlighting in particular where you have had positive impacts on businesses and people.

Think long-term and continue to sell your strengths and brand

Despite universities often focusing on MBA graduate outcomes around three years following graduation, in reality, everyone's journey is different. Although benchmarking yourself against peers can be useful, it's still worth planning your journey to be on a much longer time horizon than just a few years. Careers can span decades and are obviously highly situation dependent. What is right for one person may not be for another, and the opportunities available from person to person differ greatly. By consistently focusing on your strengths and brand, whilst continuing to learn and develop yourself, you will increase your understanding of how you can continue to improve your personal and professional situation.

Chapter Nine

Pulling it All Together

9.1 Conclusion: How to make an MBA work for you

All MBA courses teach variations on the same theme. The teaching may be of a better or worse standard and those in the cohort and your potential network may have more prestigious (or wealthy) backgrounds, but a business education should teach the fundamentals of business wherever you attend. The level of your understanding and the value of this to your own business or to a potential employer will be highly dependent on your willingness to apply the concepts in practice and pursue your professional development with an attitude of continual learning and improvement.

Excluding the super elite and US centric post-MBA roles that a select few elite MBA programmes aim to fill, you're left with normal, ambitious people trying to help improve their position in life from wherever they currently are. What makes the distinction between these remaining people, making up the majority of potential MBA students, is their ability to present themselves and their skills in a concise and impactful way. It is this ability to sell yourself as someone who can help a company do what they're setting out to achieve that will land you that job or contract, rather than a piece of paper from a university. Although the MBA certificate (or even the prospect of you having one) can open the doors, you have to find those doors, walk through them and make sure you give that company and recruiter every reason to give you that job.

This halo effect and momentum is what forms the basis of the MBA Blueprint for Success and why getting an MBA, no matter where from, can help you to achieve career success. The variables involved include what your specific career goals are, the MBA course in question and your ability to apply yourself to improving your situation. MBAs are a challenging undertaking, but it is the work invested both in and outside of the MBA that will help you translate your MBA into greater personal and professional success.

I truly hope that this book has helped you, whether you're debating putting yourself out there but need that little bit of convincing, through some additional insight and tools, or whether you know what you want and needed to understand a bit more around what you might come to find.

If you're debating whether you're capable, set out a plan to test and improve your capabilities to the required standards. If you're debating whether you can afford it, there are always options – it just might take time and commitment. If you're debating whether it's worth it for you, if you have nothing to lose, you have everything to gain. Without action, you can spend your whole life thinking and debating the pros and cons but without action you are just interested, not committed – commitment is an essential requirement for success.

Everybody has a unique situation in considering whether an MBA is right for them. Make sure that you do your research. Make sure that you consider as much as possible. Make sure that you work consistently hard. If you're willing to do more than others around you, you will see the rewards.

I wish you all the best in your journey.

A small ask from me

I wrote this book to help people and give something back, particularly the many people I've come across who could further their success if they had the insight and tools to give them more confidence.

If this book has helped you in any way, I'd really appreciate a quick review from the place you purchased it. This way, more people can understand the benefits of the book and if this is what others are looking for, the information in the book will spread further and hopefully help more people.

I truly hope you found this book insightful and beneficial and I thank you in advance for your support.

www.ingramcontent.com/pod-product-compliance
Lightning Source LLC
Chambersburg PA
CBHW021145080526
44588CB00008B/219